KT-210-445

Dubai

MINI VISITORS' GUIDE

there's more to life...
ask**explorer**.com

In a museum-like themed ambience 0f Dubai in the 1960's and with the taste of Authentic Emirati Cuisine, **AL FANAR RESTAURANT and CAFÉ** will revive the memories of Dubai when it was a small town on the shore of the Arabian Gulf.

إدارة متــاحـف الشــارقـــة
Sharjah Museums Department

BEGIN
YOUR JOURNEY OF
DISCOVERY

www.SharjahMuseums.ae

P.O. Box 39939, Sharjah, United Arab Emirates
Tel: + 971 6 5566002, Fax: + 971 6 5566003
e-mail: info@sharjahmuseums.ae

Al Eslah School

Al Mahatta Museum

Sharjah Archaeology Museum

Sharjah Art Museum

Bait Al Naboodah

Bait Sheikh Saeed Bin Hamed Al Qasimi

Sharjah Calligraphy Museum

Sharjah Maritime Museum

Sharjah Heritage Museum

Sharjah Museum of Islamic Civilization

Majlis Al Midfaa

Sharjah Car Museum

Sharjah Aquarium

Sharjah Hisn Museum

Sharjah Discovery Centre

Sharjah Science Museum

BE PART OF THE LEGEND!

MONTE CARLO BEACH CLUB

SAADIYAT

1863

2011

For over 150 years, "Société des Bains de Mer" has been taking care of its privileged guests. Come and experience the legendary Monte-Carlo Beach Club, Saadiyat – it's truly a celebration for the senses.

Bask by the picturesque poolside in personal cabanas. Marvel at the stunning Saadiyat beach. Relax at the Spa. Delight in mouthwatering cuisine from our Award winning restaurant Le Deck and dance the night away in Sea Lounge. It's a decadent privilege reserved for the few!

Monte-Carlo Beach Club, Saadiyat offers Memberships, Day Passes and a selection of unique packages. We also provide a breathtaking location and facilities ideal for your special events.

Follow us 🅵 🅴 For more information +971 2 656 3500 or info@montecarlobeachclub.ae
GPS: N 24° 33' 29.0772" E 54° 27' 4.0386" | www.montecarlobeachclub.ae

Terms & Conditions apply

MONTE-CARLO
S·B·M

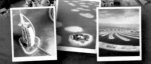

Wadi Adventure
explore your limits

Wadi Adventure is the Middle East's first man made surfing, whitewater rafting and kayaking destination located in Al Ain. We also have an airpark, climbing wall and zip line just in case your adventure fix needs topping up! With world class activities and facilities, excellent service and a backdrop like no other, your day can be as exhilarating or relaxed as you want it to be. You will also find a family swimming pool and splash pad for our younger adventurers, as well as a number of food outlets to satisfy a variety of tastes.

WADI
ADVENTURE
RAFT · KAYAK · SURF

For enquiries please call us on +971 (0)3 781 8422
email: info@wadiadventure.ae
www.wadiadventure.ae

Dubai Mini **Visitors'** Guide
ISBN – 978-9948-8518-2-0

Copyright © Explorer Group Ltd 2012
All rights reserved.

All maps © Explorer Group Ltd 2012

Front cover photograph: Burj Khalifa – Pete Maloney

Printed and bound by
Emirates Printing Press, Dubai, UAE

Explorer Publishing & Distribution
PO Box 34275, Dubai, United Arab Emirates
Phone (+971 4) 340 8805   Fax (+971 4) 340 8806
info@askexplorer.com
askexplorer.com

Welcome to the sixth edition of the *Dubai Mini Visitors' Guide*. Brimming with insider tips on everything from cultural hotspots to 'in' eateries and the best boutiques, this mini marvel has all you need to make the most out of your time in this fascinating desert metropolis.

Dubai is a dynamic city with an iconic skyline and a host of top attractions. From sandy beaches to the world's tallest tower, man-made islands to mega-malls, the City of Gold is just waiting to be discovered – and we've got it covered. Written entirely by local residents, the following pages have been passionately created by the same team that brought you the *Dubai Residents' Guide*. Packed with insider tips, our guides are updated every year to help you make the most of your trip.

For more information about Dubai and the rest of the region, plus to find out what's happening when you're in town, log onto askexplorer.com – the UAE's one-stop source for everything there is to know about Dubai and beyond.

There's more to life...
The Explorer Team

   ask**explorer**.com

Welcome...

Contents

Essentials

Welcome To Dubai

Welcome to a city of stark contrasts; of sand dunes and skyscrapers, camels and fast cars, museums and malls. Welcome to Dubai.

Whatever your reason for touching down in this desert metropolis, it's hard not to be captivated by its growth and unshakeable ambition. The world's tallest building is already here, and a slew of architectural wonderpieces and whole new communities are not far behind. Yet underneath the shiny surface there is more to Dubai than cranes and five-star cliche: you'll find Emiratis, cosmopolitan expats and sunburnt tourists, all enjoying and exploring the many aspects of a surprisingly multilayered city.

As you'd expect from a truly international destination, there is a wide scope of activities, cuisines and adventures to be had, many at prices that you wouldn't expect from the 'seven-star' headlines. Try dining in Arabic street cafes (p.232), browsing the souks (p.192) and haggling for souvenirs (p.189) to get a sense of local tradition, or sample Dubai's plethora of malls (p.200), upmarket hotels (p.66) and fine-dining restaurants for a taste of its luxury reputation.

Outside the city are a whole new set of landscapes and a more traditional way of life. Seemingly endless vistas of untouched sand dunes are just waiting to be explored, so pile into that Land Cruiser and take a tour. Further out, the East Coast of the UAE (p.136) is a haven for divers and snorkellers,

Sheikh Zayed Road

and the delights of Oman's rugged Musandam peninsula (p.142) are only an hour or so north.

Over the next few pages, descriptions of the local culture and history should provide context to your trip. Following this is the vital information you'll need to get here and stay in style, plus advice on what to do when you first arrive. The things that you really shouldn't miss start on p.20. The Exploring chapter (p.80) divides the city up, highlighting each area's best bits, such as museums, galleries and heritage sites. In Sports & Spas (p.146) you'll find out what the city has to offer for sports fans, keen golfers and those who simply prefer to be pampered. Shopping (p.180) is your detailed guide to malls, boutiques and souks, and Going Out (p.220) will help you manoeuvre your way through Dubai's increasingly impressive maze of restaurants, bars and clubs.

Culture & Heritage

Rapid change and growing multiculturalism hasn't stopped the UAE embracing a proud heritage.

Development Of Islam

Dubai's early existence is closely linked to the arrival and development of Islam in the greater Middle Eastern region. Islam developed in modern-day Saudi Arabia at the beginning of the seventh century AD with the revelations of the Quran being received by the Prophet Muhammad. Military conquests of the Middle East and North Africa enabled the Arab Empire to spread the teachings of Islam to the local Bedouin tribes. Following the Arab Empire came the Turks, the Mongols and the Ottomans, each leaving their mark on local culture.

The Trucial States

After the fall of the Muslim empires, both the British and Portuguese became interested in the area due to its strategic position between India and Europe. It also offered an opportunity to control the activities of pirates based in the region, earning it the title 'Pirate Coast'. In 1820 the British defeated the pirates and a general treaty was agreed with the local rulers, denouncing piracy. The following years witnessed a series of maritime truces, with Dubai and the other emirates accepting British protection in 1892. In Europe, the area became known as the Trucial Coast (or Trucial States), a name it retained until the departure of the British in 1971.

SHARJAH ART FOUNDATION

SHARJAH BIENNIAL 11
13 MARCH - 13 MAY 2013

CURATED BY YUKO HASEGAWA
SHARJAH, UNITED ARAB EMIRATES

REGISTER FOR MORE INFORMATION ON
VISITING HOURS AND SPECIAL EVENTS AT
REGISTER@SHARJAHART.ORG

SHARJAHART.ORG

Growing Trade

In the late 1800s Dubai's ruler, Sheikh Maktoum bin Hasher Al Maktoum, granted tax concessions to foreign traders, encouraging many to switch their operations from Iran and Sharjah to Dubai. By 1903, a British shipping line had been persuaded to use Dubai as its main port in the area, giving traders direct links with British India and other key ports. Dubai's importance as a trading hub was further enhanced by Sheikh Rashid bin Saeed Al Maktoum, father of the current ruler, who ordered the creek to be dredged to provide access for larger vessels. The city came to specialise in the import and re-export of goods, mainly gold to India, and trade became the foundation of the emirate's wealthy progression.

Independence

In 1968, Britain announced its withdrawal from the region and oversaw the proposed creation of a single state consisting of Bahrain, Qatar and the Trucial Coast. The ruling sheikhs, particularly of Abu Dhabi and Dubai, realised that by uniting forces they would have a stronger voice in the wider Middle East region. Negotiations collapsed when Bahrain and Qatar chose to become independent states. However, the Trucial Coast remained committed to forming an alliance, and in 1971 the federation of the United Arab Emirates was born.

Formation Of The UAE

The new state comprised the emirates of Dubai, Abu Dhabi, Ajman, Fujairah, Sharjah, Umm Al Quwain and, in 1972, Ras Al Khaimah. Each emirate is named after its main town.

Under the agreement, the individual emirates each retained a degree of autonomy, with Abu Dhabi and Dubai providing the most input into the federation. The leaders of the new federation elected the ruler of Abu Dhabi, HH Sheikh Zayed bin Sultan Al Nahyan, to be their president, a position he held until he passed away on 2 November 2004. His eldest son, HH Sheikh Khalifa bin Zayed Al Nahyan, was then elected to take over the presidency. Sheikh Zayed is still enormously revered in the UAE and, so far, the country has continued to witness astonishing growth under the leadership of his son, Sheikh Khalifa. With his continued focus on the development of the UAE's infrastructure, economic health and cultural contributions, the country has gone from strength to strength, furthering its international relations, safeguarding its environment and promoting its heritage.

The Discovery Of Oil

The formation of the UAE came after the discovery of huge oil reserves in Abu Dhabi in 1958. The emirate has an incredible 10% of the world's known oil reserves. This discovery dramatically transformed the emirate. In 1966, Dubai, which was already a relatively wealthy trading centre, also discovered oil. Dubai's ruler at the time, the late Sheikh Rashid bin Saeed Al Maktoum, ensured that the emirate's oil revenues were used to develop an economic and social infrastructure, which is the basis of today's modern society. His work was continued through the reign of his son and successor, Sheikh Maktoum bin Rashid Al Maktoum and by the present ruler, Sheikh Mohammed bin Rashid Al Maktoum.

Culture

Despite Dubai being a thoroughly modern metropolis, the emirate is very rooted in its traditions. Culture in Dubai is based on the Islamic customs that deeply penetrate the Arabian Peninsula and beyond. Courtesy and hospitality are highly prized virtues and visitors are likely to experience the genuine warmth and friendliness of the local people – if you meet them, of course (less than 15% of the population is Emirati). The rapid economic development over the last 30 years, that was sparked by the reign of Sheikh Zayed bin Sultan Al Nayhan (the 'father of the UAE'), has changed life in the Emirates beyond recognition. However, the country's rulers are committed to safeguarding its heritage. They are keen to promote cultural and sporting events that are representative of the UAE's traditions, such as falconry, camel racing and traditional dhow sailing. Various cultural events take place throughout the year in Dubai, as well as in the neighbouring emirate Sharjah where the Sharjah Art Foundation regularly runs art exhibitions. Generally speaking, Arabic culture, as seen through poetry, dancing, songs and traditional art, is encouraged and weddings and celebrations are wonderfully colourful occasions.

Food & Drink

Most of the Arabic food available is predominantly based on Lebanese cuisine. Common dishes are shawarma (lamb or chicken carved from a spit and served in a pita bread with salad and tahina), falafel (mashed chickpeas and sesame seeds, rolled into balls and deep fried), hummus (a creamy

Heritage Village

dip made from chickpeas and olive oil), and tabouleh (finely chopped parsley, mint and crushed wheat). There are also opportunities to sample Emirati food while in Dubai. The legacy of the UAE's trading past means that local cuisine uses a blend of ingredients imported from Asia and the Middle East. Dried limes are a common ingredient, reflecting a Persian influence; they impart a distinctively musty, tangy, sour flavour to soups and stews. Spices such as cinnamon, saffron and turmeric, along with nuts (almonds or pistachios) and dried fruit add interesting flavours to Emirati dishes.

Look out for al harees, a celebratory dish made from meat and wheat, slow-cooked in a clay pot or oven for hours, and al machboos, in which meat and rice are cooked in a stock made from local spices and dried limes. Fish is widely used in local cuisine; both freshly caught and preserved. Al madrooba is a dish which uses local salted fish prepared in a thick, buttery sauce.

Among the most famed Middle Eastern delicacies are dates and coffee. Dates are one of the few crops that thrive naturally throughout the Arab world and date palms have been cultivated in the area for around 5,000 years. The serving of traditional coffee (kahwa) is an important social ritual in the Middle East. Local coffee is mild with a distinctive taste of cardamom and saffron, and it is served black without sugar. It is considered polite to drink about three cups of the coffee when offered.

Muslims are not allowed to eat pork. In order for a restaurant to have pork on its menu, it should have a separate fridge, preparation equipment and cooking area. Supermarkets are also required to sell pork in a separate area. All meat products for Muslim consumption have to be halal, which refers to the method of slaughter.

Alcohol is also considered haram (taboo) in Islam. It is only served in licensed outlets associated with hotels (restaurants and bars), plus a few leisure venues (such as golf clubs) and clubs. Restaurants outside of hotels, that are not part of a club or association, are not permitted to serve alcohol.

Shisha

Smoking the traditional shisha (water pipe) is a popular and relaxing pastime enjoyed throughout the Middle East. Shisha pipes can be smoked with a variety of aromatic flavours, such as strawberry, grape or apple. The experience is unlike normal cigarette or cigar smoking since the tobacco and molasses are filtered through water. Contrary to what many people think, shisha tobacco contains nicotine and can be addictive. Despite ongoing rumours that smoking shisha outside will be banned in the UAE it remains hugely popular. See p.226 for some of the best spots.

Religion

Islam is the official religion of the UAE and is widely practised; however, there are people of various nationalities and religions working and living in the region side by side.

In Islam, the family unit is very important and elders are respected for their experience and wisdom. It's common for many generations to live together in the same house.

Muslims are required to pray (facing Mecca) five times a day. Most people pray at a mosque, although it's not unusual to see people kneeling by the side of the road if they are not near a place of worship. The call to prayer, transmitted through loudspeakers on the minarets of each mosque, ensures that everyone knows it's time to pray.

Friday is the Islamic holy day, and the first day of the weekend in Dubai, when most businesses close to allow people to go to the mosque to pray, and to spend time with their families. Many shops and tourist attractions have different hours of operation, opening around 14:00 after Friday prayers.

During the holy month of Ramadan, Muslims abstain from all food, drinks, cigarettes and unclean thoughts (or activities) between dawn and dusk for 30 days. In the evening, the fast is broken with the Iftar feast. All over the city, festive Ramadan tents are filled to the brim with people of all nationalities and religions enjoying shisha, traditional Arabic mezze and sweets. The timing of Ramadan is not fixed in terms of the Gregorian calendar, but depends on the lunar Islamic calendar. During Ramadan the sale of alcohol in most outlets is restricted to after dusk, while shops and parks usually open and close later. In addition, no live music or dancing is allowed. Ramadan ends with a three-day celebration and holiday called Eid Al Fitr, the feast of the breaking of the fast.

While the predominant religion in Dubai is Islam, people are freely permitted to practise other religions. The ruling family has, on numerous occasions, donated plots of land for the building of churches. Christian churches of various denominations have been built in clusters on Oud Metha Road (Map 4 B4) and in Jebel Ali, and there is a Hindu temple in Bur Dubai (Map 4 C2).

National Dress

In general, the local population wear traditional dress in public. For men this is the dishdash(a) or khandura: a white full length shirt dress, which is worn with a white or red checked headdress, known as a gutra. This is secured with a black cord (agal). Sheikhs and important businessmen may also wear a thin black or brown robe (known as a bisht or mishlah), over their dishdasha at important events. You'll sometimes see men wearing a brimless embroidered hat (kumah), which is more common in neighbouring Oman.

In public, women wear the black abaya – a long, loose robe that covers their normal clothes – plus a headscarf called a sheyla. The abaya is often of sheer, flowing fabric and may be open at the front. Some women also wear a thin black veil hiding their face and/or gloves, and some older women wear a leather mask, known as a burkha, which covers the nose, brow and cheekbones. Underneath the abaya, women traditionally wear a long tunic over loose fitting trousers (sirwal), which are normally heavily embroidered and fitted at the wrists and ankles.

Cross Culture

The Sheikh Mohammed Centre for Cultural Understanding (p.88) was established to help bridge the gaps between cultures and give visitors and residents a clearer appreciation of the Emirati way of life. It organises tours of Jumeirah Mosque (p.113), one of the few in the UAE open to non-Muslims (cultures.ae).

Modern Dubai

The City of Gold has transformed into a thriving metropolis with an iconic skyline and ambitious future plans.

Dubai's rise to prominence has taken place at an astounding pace. Since the discovery of oil in the 1950s, the city has transformed beyond recognition. The pace of development over the past decade or so has been particularly noteworthy, with a near constant stream of announcements for new billion-dollar developments. After a temporary slowdown in 2009 in the wake of the global financial crisis, development is now firmly back on track: several amazing projects have already been completed and the city's heartbeat is once again truly palpable. While development is still continuing on some of the more ambitious projects, it's unquestionable that Dubai has transformed into a regional metropolis with its eyes firmly fixed on the future.

People & Economy

There are an estimated 150 nationalities living in Dubai and the population has grown multifold over the past few decades: according to a national census, the population in 1968 was 58,971 – by 2012 it is estimated to have ticked over the 2 million mark. Expats make up more than 80% of the population. Nearly 75% of expat residents hail from the Asian subcontinent, many of whom work on the construction

View of Emirates Towers from DIFC

of the city's massive skyscrapers that have come to define it, while the other expats represent various nationalities from all over the world to make a truly global community. Dubai's economy has been weaning itself off oil dependence for the last few decades. Whereas 20 years ago oil revenues accounted for around half of Dubai's GDP, the hydrocarbons now contributes just a few percentage points. Today, the main contributors include trade, transport, real estate, tourism and finance, with the Dubai International Financial Centre (DIFC) alone contributing around 3.6% in 2010.

Tourism

Dubai is well ahead of many other cities in the Middle East in terms of travel and tourism. The development of high-end hotels and much-publicised visitor attractions has made Dubai a popular holiday destination for tourists from near and far. In 2011, the number of hotel guests staying in Dubai increased by around 11% to more than 9 million, while annual passenger traffic through Dubai International Airport grew by around 8% to over 50 million. Tourists from Britain, India, Iran, Saudi Arabia and the US are among the most frequent visitors, with more than 700,000 Brits alone arriving in the emirate in 2010.

New Developments

Until 2009, Dubai's booming economy meant that for every record-breaking mega development that was completed, three new ones were announced. In the wake of the global economic slow-down of that year, some projects fell behind their original schedules and others have been put on hold. This said, several high-profile projects have been completed and work on many others is going ahead. The Palm Jumeirah (p.118) and the iconic Burj Khalifa (p.21) are among the best examples of fully finalised developments that have come to symbolise Dubai. The city's notorious traffic jams have eased following the completion of the Dubai Metro (p.56) and work is underway to build a separate tramline. On the sporting front, several facilities are now open at Dubai Sports City (dubaisportscity.ae), while the annual Dubai World Cup (p.54) takes place at the impressive Meydan Racecourse.

Clockwise from top left: Meydan Racecourse, Burj Khalifa, Dubai Sports City

Dubai Checklist

01 Ski Dubai

This indoor slope, jutting out of the MoE (p.207), has five 'real snow' runs, a nursery slope, a selection of rails and jumps, resident penguins, and a snow park where kids can roll around in the white stuff. Lessons are available, and there's a cafe halfway up the piste.

02 At The Top, Burj Khalifa

A visit to the world's tallest building is a must. Ride the super-fast elevator to the 124th floor's viewing deck for 360° views across Dubai. Alternatively, book a table at At.mosphere – the world's highest restaurant (p.253).

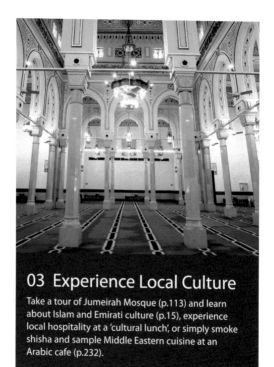

03 Experience Local Culture

Take a tour of Jumeirah Mosque (p.113) and learn about Islam and Emirati culture (p.15), experience local hospitality at a 'cultural lunch', or simply smoke shisha and sample Middle Eastern cuisine at an Arabic cafe (p.232).

04 Tackle The Dunes

A trip to the desert is a must during your stay in Dubai. Surfing over the dunes in a car at impossible angles is great fun – as is a camel ride, eating your fill at a barbecue and learning how to belly dance. Tour operators are plentiful and professional. See p.145.

05 Sample The Souks

Still an essential part of life for many people, Dubai's souks are a welcome slice of tradition. Check out the Spice Souk (p.198), the colourful textile souk in Bur Dubai (p.199), the Fish Market in Deira and the world-renowned Gold Souk (p.194).

06 Burgeoning Buildings

Splash out on afternoon tea at the Skyview Bar (p.316) at the iconic, sail-shaped Burj Al Arab hotel (p.69). The other burj, the Burj Khalifa (p.21), is the world's tallest building and as such a monument to Dubai's sky-high ambition.

Dubai Checklist

07 Take A Bus Tour

View the city from the upper floor of a double-decker bus, learning some fascinating facts about Dubai along the way. The Big Bus Tours (p.145) allows you to hop on and off at various attractions, while the amphibious Wonder Bus also takes to water (p.145).

08 Hit The Malls

Dubai does shopping bigger and better than most. So whether it's to beat the heat or browse the boutiques, you won't be short of options. See p.180 for a full guide to the city's shopping hotspots, including one of the largest malls in the world, The Dubai Mall (p.204).

09 Explore Old Dubai

Wander among traditional Arabic windtower houses in the beautifully restored Bastakiya area (p.86). Stroll through the city's history at the nearby Dubai Museum (p.87) and learn about traditional trades at the Heritage & Diving Village on the banks of the creek (p.92).

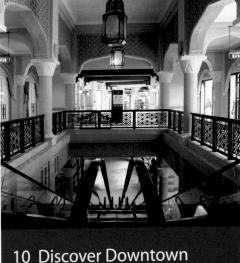

10 Discover Downtown

Head to Downtown Dubai for trendy cafes, buzzing bars, chic restaurants and scintillating shopping opportunities at Souk Al Bahar (p.197) and The Dubai Mall (p.204). The dancing Dubai Fountain (p.100) is a light, music and water spectacle not to be missed.

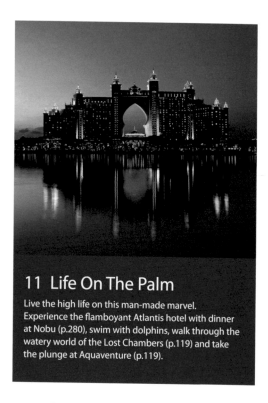

11 Life On The Palm

Live the high life on this man-made marvel.
Experience the flamboyant Atlantis hotel with dinner
at Nobu (p.280), swim with dolphins, walk through the
watery world of the Lost Chambers (p.119) and take
the plunge at Aquaventure (p.119).

12 Life's A Beach

There's no shortage of sand in Dubai and with kilometres of aquamarine sea beckoning, spending time at the beach is a must. Relax on the golden sands at Jumeirah Beach Park (p.113) or enjoy exclusive facilities at a beachside hotel (p.66).

For Adrenaline Junkies

Take a bird's eye view of the growing metropolis while parasailing (p.152) at one of the many beachside hotels or treat yourself to a helicopter tour.

Dune bashing is a great way to clear the cobwebs and see some spectacular desert vistas. If you go with a tour group (p.144), sand skiing or boarding might be on offer too. If you want to get behind the wheel, you'll find dune buggies and quad biking on the road to Hatta (p.138). If it's too hot then head to Dubai Autodrome (dubaiautodrome.com) for a karting race around the 1.2km track or the 500m indoor circuit.

To really get your pulse racing, why not take a dip with the sharks at Dubai Aquarium (p.99)? Novice and experienced divers can take the plunge with the aquarium's 33,000 inhabitants under the supervision of qualified instructors.

For Big Spenders

Dubai is a shopper's paradise offering everything from market stall haggling to haute couture. If labels are your thing, The Boulevard at Emirates Towers is home to several designers but for anything you can't find there try the exclusive boutiques at Wafi (p.212). Fashionistas will love the collections along Fashion Avenue at The Dubai Mall (p.204) where they can rest their heels at the Armani Cafe post-purchase.

For Culture Buffs

Delve beneath its glamorous exterior and you'll find the Dubai of old. Sample local cuisine (p.227), hang out in shisha cafes (p.226), explore the souks (p.192), travel on an abra

Fairmont Dubai

(p.65), visit the dhow wharfage on the Deira side of the Creek, hunt for authentic souvenirs (p.189), and uncover the history at Dubai Museum (p.87). Meanwhile, the art and gallery scene is keeping pace with the skyscrapers. Check out the latest exhibitions at The Third Line (p.131) and The Jam Jar (p.129), or to really immerse yourself in the art world, stay at XVA, a funky gallery and hotel in Bastakiya (p.86).

For Foodies

Dubai offers an eclectic mix of American fastfood staples, Lebanese street cafes and fine-dining hotel restaurants, but while in town it is the delicious Arabic food that should

be top of your list. Try shawarmas, falafel, hummus, and tabouleh, all washed down with the finest fresh juices. Try Al Fanar (p.247) for authentic Emirati cuisine and see p.227 for the pick of the rest.

For Water Babies

From relaxing at the hotel pool and Jumeirah Beach Park (p.113) to diving, snorkelling, sailing and watersports (p.158), there are plenty of opportunities to cool off in the water. Make your own mind up in the battle of the waterparks, choosing between Arabian-themed Wild Wadi (p.120) and the Atlantis hotel's hair-raising Aquaventure (p.119).

For Architecture Admirers

An architect's playground, Dubai is home to many staggering feats of construction. From the sail-shaped Burj Al Arab (p.69) to the world's tallest building, the Burj Khalifa (p.21), and the teetering towers of Dubai Marina (p.104), there are scores of striking skylines waiting to be captured on camera.

For Party People

Sip cocktails to a Balearic soundtrack as the sun sinks into the Arabian Gulf at 360° (p.302) or warm up at beach bar favourite Barasti (p.304). Trawl the stylish bars of Souk Al Bahar (p.197), then dance under the stars at open-sky nightclub The Lodge (p.309), or strut your stuff with the designer set at the Cavalli Club (p.308). From the luxurious to the laidback, Dubai's nightlife offerings are surprisingly diverse.

Atmospheric Old Town

Visiting Dubai

The UAE warmly welcomes visitors, but has a few rules and regulations that require extra attention. Read on for the vital information.

Getting There

Dubai International Airport (DXB) is an important global travel hub, handling more than 50 million passengers in 2011. Currently, this makes it the fourth busiest airport in the world and flight connections exist to over 220 destinations. Terminal 1 handles major international airlines; Terminal 3 is exclusively used by Dubai's Emirates; while Terminal 2 is home to budget operator flydubai and other low-cost carriers, as well as charter flights. The Terminal 3 experience is seamless with ample shopping opportunities, spas and chill-out gardens.

Airport Info

The main phone number for Dubai International Airport is 04 224 5555. For up-to-date flight information call 04 216 6666 and for baggage services, including lost property, call 04 224 5383.

Terminals 1 and 2 tend to get busier and queuing for check-in and passport control can take a while during peak hours. Generally speaking, the airport is clean and modern, facilities are good, and there's a huge duty free section in Terminals 1 and 3.

Airport Transfer

If you booked your break through a hotel or travel agency, it's likely that pick-up from the airport will be included.

If not, the Metro (p.56) connects the airport to destinations the length of Dubai directly from Terminals 1 and 3, or you could grab a cab. The taxi stand is straight in front of you as you leave the arrivals hall in all terminals. Taxis leaving from the airport charge an extra Dhs.25 so it costs around Dhs.50

Airlines		
Air Arabia	06 508 8888	airarabia.com
Air France	800 23 823	airfrance.ae
American Airlines	04 316 6116	aa.com
British Airways	800 0441 3322	britishairways.com
Emirates	04 214 4444	emirates.com
Etihad Airways	02 511 0000	etihadairways.com
flydubai	04 301 0800	flydubai.com
Gulf Air	04 316 6442	gulfairco.com
KLM Royal Dutch Airlines	800 556	klm.com
Lufthansa	04 373 9100	lufthansa.com
Oman Air	04 351 8080	oman-air.com
Qatar Airways	04 229 2229	qatarairways.com
Royal Brunei Airlines	04 334 4884	bruneiair.com
Royal Jet Group	02 575 7000	royaljetgroup.com
Singapore Airlines	04 316 6888	singaporeair.com
South African Airways	04 397 0766	flysaa.com
United Airlines	800 441 5492	united.com
Virgin Atlantic	04 406 0600	virgin-atlantic.com

for a journey to the hotels of Sheikh Zayed Road and the Downtown area (p.98) or up to Dhs.90 to Dubai Marina and the beach hotels of JBR (p.104).

An airport bus runs to and from the airport every 30 minutes, 24 hours a day. There are a number of loop routes: C1 runs to Satwa, while the 88 goes to Nakheel Metro Station. Log on to wojhati.rta.ae to plan your journey.

Visas & Customs

Requirements vary depending on your country of origin and it's wise to check the regulations before departure. GCC nationals (Bahrain, Kuwait, Qatar, Oman and Saudi Arabia) do not need a visa to enter Dubai. Citizens from many other countries get an automatic visa upon arrival at the airport (see info box below for the full list). The entry visa is valid for

Visa On Arrival

Citizens of the following countries receive an automatic visa on arrival: Andorra, Australia, Austria, Belgium, Brunei, Denmark, Finland, France, Germany, Greece, Hong Kong, Iceland, Ireland, Italy, Japan, Liechtenstein, Luxembourg, Malaysia, Monaco, The Netherlands, New Zealand, Norway, Portugal, San Marino, Singapore, South Korea, Spain, Sweden, Switzerland, United Kingdom, United States of America and Vatican City.

60 days, although you can renew for a further 30 days. For those travelling onwards to a destination other than that of the original departure, a special transit visa (up to 96 hours) may be obtained free of charge through selected airlines.

Certain medications, including codeine, Temazepam and Prozac, are banned even though they are freely available in other countries. High-profile cases have highlighted the UAE's zero tolerance to drugs. Even a miniscule quantity in your possession could result in a lengthy jail term. Bags will also be scanned to ensure you have no offending magazines or DVDs.

Dos & Don'ts

The UAE is one of the most tolerant and liberal states in the region, but as a guest in a Muslim country you should act accordingly. Lewd and drunken behaviour is not only disrespectful but can lead to arrest and detention. There is also zero tolerance to drinking alcohol and driving (p.44). Women should be aware that revealing clothing can attract unwanted attention, so very short dresses and strapless tops should be avoided outside of beach areas. Malls have put up signs making it clear that inappropriate clothing and public displays of affection are not allowed. It is courteous to ask permission before photographing people, particularly women. With prices for cigarettes low, smoking is very common. However, new laws have banned lighting up in malls and some restaurants so it's best to check the policy before striking up.

Local Knowledge

Climate

Dubai has a subtropical and arid climate. Sunny blue skies and high temperatures can be expected most of the year. Rainfall is infrequent, averaging only 25 days per year, mainly in winter (December to March). Summer temperatures can hit a soaring 48°C (118°F) and with humidity well above 60% it can make for uncomfortable conditions from June to September. The most pleasant time to visit Dubai is during the cooler winter months when average temperatures range between 30°C and 14°C, perfect for comfortable days on the beach and long, lingering evenings outside. For up-to-date weather forecasts, see dubaiairport.com/dubaimet.

Time

The UAE is four hours ahead of UTC (Universal Coordinated Time – formerly known as GMT). There is no altering of clocks for daylight saving in the summer, so when Europe and North America lose an hour, the time in the UAE stays the same. Most offices and schools are closed on Fridays and Saturdays. This causes few problems for visitors but be aware that the Metro and some shops don't open until later on Fridays.

Electricity & Water

The electricity supply is 220/240 volts and 50 cycles. Most hotel rooms and villas use the three-pin plug that is used in the UK. Adaptors are widely available and only cost a few dirhams. Tap water is desalinated sea water and is perfectly safe to drink although most people choose mineral water because it tastes better. Bottled water is cheap, especially local brands such as Masafi. Bottled water, both local and imported, is served in hotels and restaurants.

Money

Credit and debit cards are widely accepted around Dubai. Foreign currencies and travellers' cheques can be exchanged in licensed exchange offices, banks and hotels. Cash is preferred in the souks, markets and in smaller shops, and paying in cash will help your bargaining power. If you've hired a car, be aware that only cash is accepted at petrol pumps.

The monetary unit is the dirham (Dhs.), which is divided into 100 fils. The currency is also referred to as AED (Arab Emirate dirham). Notes come in denominations of Dhs.5 (brown), Dhs.10 (green), Dhs.20 (light blue), Dhs.50 (purple), Dhs.100 (pink), Dhs.200 (yellowy-brown), Dhs.500 (blue) and Dhs.1,000 (browny-purple).

The dirham has been pegged to the US dollar since 1980, at a mid rate of $1 to Dhs.3.6725.

Tipping

Tipping practices are similar across hotels, restaurants and bars in Dubai, with tips being shared between all of the staff. Many places add a service charge onto the bill but no one really knows if this actually goes to the staff so many people add a little extra. The usual amount to tip is 10%. Many restaurant bills in hotels automatically come with 10% municipality tax and 10% service charge included, so check the total amount carefully. In a taxi it is standard, but not compulsory, to round up the fare to the nearest Dhs.5.

Language

Arabic is the official language of the UAE, although English, Hindi, Malayalam and Urdu are commonly spoken. You can easily get by with English, but if you can throw in a couple of Arabic words here and there, you're likely to receive at least a smile.

Basic Arabic

General

Yes	na'am
No	la
Please	min fadlak (m)/min fadliki (f)
Thank you	shukran
Praise be to God	al-hamdu l-illah
God willing	in shaa'a l-laah

Greetings

Greeting (peace be upon you)	as-salaamu alaykom
Greeting (in reply)	wa alaykom is salaam
Good morning	sabah il-khayr
Good morning (in reply)	sabah in-nuwr
Good evening	masa il-khayr
Good evening (in reply)	masa in-nuwr
Hello	marhaba
Hello (in reply)	marhabtayn
How are you?	kayf haalak (m)/kayf haalik (f)
Fine, thank you	zayn, shukran (m)/zayna, shukran (f)

Local Knowledge

Welcome	ahlan wa sahlan
Goodbye	ma is-salaama

Introduction

My name is...	ismiy...
What is your name?	shuw ismak (m) / shuw ismik (f)
Where are you from?	min wayn inta (m) / min wayn (f)

Questions

How many / much?	kam?
Where?	wayn?
When?	mataa?
Which?	ayy?
How?	kayf?
What?	shuw?
Why?	laysh?
And	wa

Numbers

Zero	sifr
One	waahad
Two	ithnayn
Three	thalatha
Four	arba'a
Five	khamsa
Six	sitta
Seven	saba'a
Eight	thamaanya
Nine	tiss'a
Ten	ashara

Crime & Safety

Pickpocketing and crimes against tourists are a rarity in Dubai, and visitors can enjoy feeling safe and unthreatened in most places around town. A healthy degree of caution should still be exercised, however, and most hotels offer safes for keeping your valuables and travel documents locked away.

To avoid a great deal of hassle if your personal documents go missing, make sure you keep one photocopy with friends or family back home and one copy in your hotel safe. Dubai Police (see left) will advise you on a course of action in the case of a loss or theft. If you've lost something in a taxi, call the taxi company (see the last page of this book). If you lose your passport, your next stop should be your embassy or consulate (see the pull-out map). With high accident rates, extra caution should be taken on Dubai's roads, whether navigating

Police

Dubai Police's Department for Tourist Security is a helpful, friendly service should you run in to any trouble during your stay. For assistance, call the toll free number (800 4438) or visit the Dubai Police website, dubaipolice.gov. ae. There's a separate hotline for reporting problems on the beach, including sexual harassment or annoyance by quad bikes (04 266 1228). For other emergency services call 999 for police or ambulance and 997 for fire.

View towards Downtown Dubai

Local Knowledge

the streets on foot or in a vehicle. Use designated pedestrian crossings wherever possible (jaywalking is actually illegal), and make sure all cars are going to stop before you cross. For more info on road safety, see p.64. There is zero tolerance towards drink driving, even after one pint, and if you're caught you can expect a spell in prison. With thousands of low-fare taxis available there is no excuse or need.

Accidents & Emergencies

If you witness an accident or need an ambulance in an emergency situation, the number to call is 999. For urgent medical care, there are several private hospitals with excellent A&E facilities. The American Hospital Dubai (ahdubai.com) is among the biggest and most trusted – see the pull-out map for listings and contact details. Anyone can receive emergency treatment in government hospitals but note that charges apply to those without Dubai health cards. For general non-emergency medical care, most hospitals have a walk-in clinic where you can simply turn up for a consultation with a physicist; for example, Medcare (medcarehospital.com) has several clinics across Dubai.

People With Disabilities

Dubai is starting to consider the needs of visitors with special needs more seriously although, in general, facilities are limited, particularly at older tourist attractions. When asking if a location has wheelchair access, make sure it really does – an escalator is considered 'wheelchair access' in some instances. That said, Dubai International Airport

is well equipped for travellers with special needs, with automatic doors, large lifts and all counters accessible by wheelchair users, as well as several services such as porters, special transportation and quick check-in to avoid long queues. Dubai Transport has a few specially modified taxis for journeys from the airport and around town, and all Metro stations are designed to give easy access to wheelchair users. Metro stations also have tactile floor routes for visually impaired people. Most of the newer malls have wheelchair access and five-star and recently built hotels should offer accessible rooms for visitors with special needs.

Telephone & Internet

It is possible to buy temporary (three-month) SIM cards for mobile phones that work on a pay-as-you go basis. Etisalat's 'Ahlan' package costs Dhs.60. This includes Dhs.25 credit, and lasts for 90 days with an extra 30 day grace period when you can receive calls. It is available from the airport and malls. Alternatively, you can buy du's pre-paid package online (du. ae) or at its outlets in most malls. For Dhs.55 you will get a welcome bonus of Dhs.25, usage

Public Toilets

You will find plenty of clean, modern, western-style toilets in the malls but there is a distinct lack of public bathrooms on shopping streets. Facilities on open beaches tend to be pretty basic, so carrying tissues will come in handy.

Deira Creekside

bonus of Dhs.100, and lifetime validity (provided minimum top-ups are made). You can easily buy top-up cards for both packages from supermarkets, newsagents and petrol stations. Mobile phone numbers in the UAE begin with a prefix of 050, 052, 055 or 056. Wi-Fi is available in many hotel rooms. Most five-star accommodation also includes the use of a business centre (sometimes for a fee) with computers and internet access. Many cafes around Dubai offer free Wi-Fi; some of the hotspots include Starbucks, Caribou Coffee and cafes in Mall Of The Emirates (p.207) and The Dubai Mall (p.204).

Media & Further Reading

Newspapers & Magazines

There are several English language newspapers in Dubai. You will see free copies of *7Days* on display; this daily tabloid contains international news alongside cinema listings and gossip. *The National*, *Khaleej Times* and *Gulf News* (all Dhs.3) are broadsheets that offer local and international current affairs with regular supplements. UK broadsheet *The Times* publishes an international edition, which is available daily for Dhs.10 in most supermarkets. Larger supermarkets and news agents also stock copies of international newspapers from the *Financial Times* and *Wall Street Journal* to *Le Figaro* and *La Repubblica*.

For magazines and lifestyle titles, there are plenty of local options, including a range of Middle Eastern editions of international titles that are produced in Dubai. These include *Harper's Bazaar*, *OK!*, *Hello!* and *Grazia* for all the regular gossip and news, with

More Info?

To find out more about what's going on in Dubai, check out askexplorer.com, Explorer's community driven hub for news, events and local information from A to Z. For the lowdown on all there is to experience across the whole country, grab a copy of *The Ultimate UAE Explorer*. If you fancy getting behind the wheel on the stunning sand dunes, *The UAE Off-Road Explorer* is essential reading. These titles and many more are available at askexplorer.com/shop.

extras from around the region. Bookshops such as Borders stock a good selection, as do most larger supermarkets. Many of the major, international glossy magazines are also available in Dubai (although as they're imported from the US or Europe, you can expect to pay at least twice the normal cover price). All international titles are examined and, where necessary, censored to ensure that they don't offend the country's moral codes.

Television

Most hotel rooms will have satellite or cable, broadcasting a mix of local and international channels. You'll find MTV, major news stations and some BBC programming, in addition to the standard hotel room information loop. For a slice of local flavour, check out local stations City7, Dubai TV and Dubai One, all of which broadcast Arabic soap operas, talkshows and American sitcoms in addition to local news programmes.

Radio

Catering for Dubai's multinational inhabitants, there are stations broadcasting in English, French, Hindi, Malayalam and Urdu. Daily schedules can be found in newspapers. Of the English-speaking stations, there is a good range to choose from. Tune into Dubai 92 (92.0 FM), Radio 1 (104.1 FM), Radio 2 (99.3 FM), The Coast (103.2 FM) and Virgin Radio (104.4 FM) for music or Dubai Eye (103.8 FM) for talk radio and sport. All stations broadcast regular news and travel updates. You can pick up BBC World Service in English and Arabic (87.9 FM).

Public Holidays & Annual Events

Public Holidays

The Islamic calendar starts from the year 622AD, the year of Prophet Muhammad's migration (Hijra) from Mecca to Al Madinah. Hence, the Islamic year is called the Hijri year and dates are followed by AH (AH stands for Anno Hegirae, meaning 'after the year of the Hijra'). As some holidays are based on the sighting of the moon and do not have fixed dates on the Hijri calendar, Islamic holidays are more often than not confirmed less than 24 hours in advance. The main Muslim festivals are Eid Al Fitr (the festival of the breaking of the fast, which marks the end of Ramadan) and Eid Al Adha (the festival of the sacrifice, which marks the end of the pilgrimage to Mecca). Mawlid Al Nabee is the holiday celebrating Prophet Muhammad's birthday, and Lailat Al Mi'raj celebrates the Prophet's ascension into heaven.

In general, public holidays are unlikely to disrupt a visit to Dubai, except that shops may open a bit later and on a few specific days, alcohol is not served. During Ramadan, food and beverages cannot be consumed in public during the day;

Public Holidays 2012-14

	2012	2013	2014
New Year's Day (Fixed)	Jan 1	Jan 1	Jan 1
Mawlid Al Nabee (Moon)	Feb 4	Jan 24	Jan 13
Lailat Al Mi'raj (Moon)	Jun 17	Jun 6	May 26
Eid Al Fitr (2-3 days; Moon)	Aug 19	Aug 8	Jul 28
Eid Al Adha (2-3 days; Moon)	Oct 26	Oct 15	Oct 4
Islamic New Year's Day (Moon)	Nov 15	Nov 4	Oct 25
UAE National Day (Fixed)	Dec 2	Dec 2	Dec 2

however, in most tourist hotels, there are special areas which serve diners all day long. Smoking and chewing gum are also prohibited, and you should dress more conservatively than usual. These rules apply to Muslims and non-Muslims alike.

Annual Events

Throughout the year, Dubai hosts an impressive array of events, from the world's richest horse race and international tennis to well-respected jazz and film festivals. Many attract thousands of international visitors and tickets often sell out quickly.

Dubai Shopping Festival   January to February
Various Locations   dubaievents.ae
Dubai Shopping Festival is a great time to be in the city with bargains galore for shoppers and entertainers, prize draws and kids' shows held in participating malls.

Omega Dubai Desert Classic   January to February
Emirates Golf Club, Emirates Living
dubaidesertclassic.com
A longstanding PGA European Tour fixture and a highly popular event among Dubai's expat golfing community.

Dubai Duty Free Tennis Championships   February
The Aviation Club, Al Garhoud
dubaidutyfreetennischampionships.com
Firmly established on the ATP and WTP circuit, this major tournament attracts the world's top men's and women's seeds.

Skywards Dubai International Jazz Festival

February

Dubai Media City, Al Sufouh 1   dubaijazzfest.com

The Jazz Festival attracts a broad range of artists from all around the world to a chilled and pleasant setting in Dubai Media City.

Abu Dhabi Desert Challenge

March

Empty Quarter, Abu Dhabi   abudhabidesertchallenge.ae

This high-profile motorsport event attracts some of the world's top rally drivers and bike riders.

Dubai World Cup

March

Meydan Racecourse, Meydan   dubaiworldcup.com

The buzzing atmosphere at the richest horse race in the world (last year's total prize money was more than $20 million) makes it one of the year's big social occasions.

Seeing Stars

Large-scale concerts and other events attracting top name celebrities are regularly hosted in the UAE. The past few years have seen just about everyone from Kylie to Andrea Bocelli perform live in Dubai or a short hop away in Abu Dhabi. Other fixtures have seen Train, Macy Gray, James Blunt and the late Amy Winehouse strut their stuff, while superstar DJs Fat Boy Slim, Paul Oakenfold and Bob Sinclair have taken to the decks. Check out askexplorer.com to find out what's on when you're in town.

Camel Racing
November to March

Meydan Racecourse, Nad Al Sheba   meydan.ae

This popular local sport is serious business, with racing camels changing hands for as much as Dhs.10 million. Races take place during winter from 07:00 to 08:30. Admission is free.

Formula 1 Etihad Airways Abu Dhabi Grand Prix
November

Yas Marina Circuit, Abu Dhabi   formula1.com

Racing fans delight in this F1 weekend: the event usually has a number of big name concerts to top up the experience.

DP World Tour Championship
November

Jumeirah Golf Estates   dpworldtourchampionship.com

The final fixture of the Race To Dubai tournament in which the world's best have a shot at a share of the $7.5 million prize fund.

Emirates Airlines Dubai Rugby Sevens
November

The Sevens   dubairugby7s.com

Over 130,000 people come to watch top international and local Gulf teams battle it out. With friendly rivalry and prizes for fancy dress, the party carries on until the small hours.

Dubai International Film Festival
December

Madinat Jumeirah, Al Sufouh   dubaifilmfest.com

A showcase of Hollywood, international and regional films with screenings in cinemas across the city.

Getting Around

With the expanding Metro system, air-conditioned buses and cheap taxis, travelling round Dubai is easier than you think.

You may have heard horror stories about arduous commutes, sticky strolls in the summer and terrifying taxi journeys, but it is surprisingly simple, and pretty cheap, to get around Dubai. Public transport took its first real leap forward in 2009 with the launch of Dubai Metro. Cheap and plentiful taxis are still a popular method of transport, but don't overlook the even cheaper bus routes; it's even possible to explore some areas on foot during the cooler winter months. If you prefer to be in control then hiring a car is a great way to get out of the city but bear in mind the variable driving standards of many motorists. If you're keen to get off the road then take a trip on a traditional abra or modern water bus. Many people use them for daily trips and they offer a fresh perspective on the city.

Metro

The ultra-modern Dubai Metro opened in September 2009, bringing public transport to the masses. The Red Line runs from Rashidiya to the airport, and down Sheikh Zayed Road – passing the financial district, Downtown, Al Barsha and Dubai Marina – before terminating at Danube Group (see pull-out map). All 29 stations on the Red Line were open by 2010 and in September 2011, 18 new stations were also open on the

Dubai Metro network

Arabian Gulf

Salahudin
Abu Baker Al Siddque
Abu Hail
Al Quiadah
Stadium
Al Nahda
Airport Freezone
Al Qusais 1
Etisalat
Terminal 1
Terminal 3
Emirates
Rashidiya

Baniyas
Palm Deira
Al Ras
Al Ghubaiba
Union
Al Fahidi
Al Riqqa
BurJuman
Deira City Centre
Al Karama
GGICO
Al Jafilya
Oud
Healthcare
Trade Centre
Metha
City
Jaddaf
Emirates Twrs
Creek
Financial Centre
Burj Khalifa/Dubai Mall

Business Bay

Noor Islamic Bank

First Gulf Bank
Mall of the Emirates
Sharaf DG
Dubai Internet City

Nakheel
Dubai Marina
Jumeirah Lakes Towers
Nakheel Harbour & Tower
Ibn Battuta

Energy

DANUBE

JAFZA/Limitless

101102

Green Line, which runs from Al Qusais on the Sharjah border to Jaddaf. Trains run from around 06:00 to 24:00 on weekdays, and until 01:00 during the weekend, at intervals of 3 to 4 minutes at peak times; on Fridays, the service starts at 13:00. Each train has a section for women and children only, and a first or Gold class cabin. The fare structure operates as a pay-as-you-go system in which you touch your prepaid Nol card in and out at stations (p.59).

Following the opening of more stations, the Metro is now a fully viable means of getting around the city. However, if you are staying in one of the beachside hotels, you will need to make use of a feeder bus (or taxi) to access the station. Check the RTA's journey planner (see p.59) for travel options or, if you are short for time, it's probably best to hop in a cab. This said, the metro is also a fantastic way to do sightseeing: the majority of the route is above ground, meaning you'll get a bird's eye view of the city from one end to the other.

A separate monorail runs the length of Palm Jumeirah from the Gateway Towers station on the mainland to Atlantis hotel. Trains run daily from 10:00 to 22:00 and cost Dhs.15 for a single fare or Dhs.25 for a return.

Work has also begun on a tramline along Al Sufouh Road which will eventually service Dubai Marina, Media City and Knowledge Village, linking to the Metro system and the Palm Monorail.

Bus

There are dozens of bus routes servicing the main residential and commercial areas of Dubai. The buses and bus shelters are air-conditioned, modern and clean, although they can be rather crowded at peak times. Efforts are being made to display better timetables and route plans at bus stops to encourage people to use buses. The main bus stations are near the Gold Souk in Deira and on Al Ghubaiba Road in Bur Dubai. Buses run at regular intervals until around midnight and a handful of Nightliner buses operate from 23:30 till 06:00. The front three rows of seats on all buses are reserved for women and children only. Cash is not accepted so you need to purchase a Nol card (see below) before boarding. Call the RTA (800 9090) or check the website (rta.ae) for comprehensive route plans, timetables and fares.

Nol Card

Introduced with the opening of the Metro, Nol cards are convenient, rechargeable travel cards which can be used to pay for public transport and street car parking. Single journeys start at Dhs.1.80 for up to 3km, rising to Dhs.5.80 for travel across two or more zones. The red Nol card is a paper ticket aimed at tourists and occasional users. It can be charged for up to 10 journeys, but is only valid on one type of transport at a time – bus, Metro or water bus. The silver Nol card costs Dhs.20, including Dhs.14

Journey Planner

The best way to work out your public transport options is to use the Road & Transport Authority's (RTA) online journey planner at http://wojhati.rta.ae (wojhati is Arabic for journey planner). For further assistance, call the RTA on 800 9090.

credit. It can be recharged up to Dhs.500 and is a better option if you plan to use different types of public transport or travel extensively while in town. The gold card is identical to the silver, except that holders are charged first class prices (usually double the standard fare) and can travel in the Gold class cabins of the Metro. Nol cards can be purchased and topped up at Metro and bus stations and at selected stores including Carrefour and Spinneys.

Cycling

A lot of care is needed when cycling in the UAE as some drivers pay little attention to other cars, much less cyclists. Also, in the hotter months, you'll be pedalling in 45°C heat. If you are visiting in winter and want to cycle, head to Creek Park (p.124) where you can rent a bike and explore in safety.

Driving & Car Hire

It's a brave individual who gets behind the wheel in Dubai. Drivers are erratic, roads are constantly changing and the

Car Rental Agencies

Avis	04 295 7121	avisuaecarhire.com
Budget Rent-a-Car	04 295 6667	budget-uae.com
Diamond Lease	04 343 4330	diamondlease.com
EuroStar Rent-a-Car	04 266 1117	eurostarrental.com
Hertz	800 437 89	hertz-uae.com
National Car Rental	04 283 2020	national-me.com
Thrifty Car Rental	800 4694	thriftyuae.com

ASCOTT
PARK PLACE
DUBAI

Exclusive Global Living in the Heart of Dubai

tay at along the exclusive Sheikh Zayed Road, home to Dubai's most valuable real estate. Ascott Park Place
ubai provides luxury serviced residences overlooking breathtaking views of the city with comprehensive
ervices and modern facilities in the iconic Park Place Tower. After a long day, take a dip in our 40-metre
mperature controlled swimming pool, work out in our state-of-the-art gymnasium or relax in our steam &
auna rooms. Live the exclusive life, only at Ascott Park Place Dubai. **Because life is about living.**

Managed by

THE
ASCOTT
LIMITED

A Member of CapitaLand

r further information and global reservations, please visit www.the-ascott.com or call +971 4310 8503

scott Park Place Dubai is managed by The Ascott Limited, a member of CapitaLand. It is the largest global serviced residence owner-operator in
Asia Pacific, Europe and the Gulf region, managing the Ascott, Citadines and Somerset brands in over 70 cities across more than 20 countries.

traffic jams can be enduring. On the bright side, most cars are automatic, which makes city driving a lot easier. If you are a confident driver, you'll probably find that driving in Dubai looks much worse than it is in practice. Expect the unexpected and use your mirrors and indicators. Weekends, especially Fridays, are much clearer on the roads but during the week traffic heading into Dubai from Deira in the morning and out in the evening can be horrendous. Driving is on the right hand side of the road.

International car rental companies, plus a few local firms, can be found in Dubai. Prices range from Dhs.80 a day for smaller cars to Dhs.1,000 for limousines. Comprehensive insurance is essential; make sure that it includes personal accident coverage. To rent a car, you are required to produce a copy of your passport, a valid international driving licence and a credit card. The rental company may be able to help arrange international or temporary local licences for visitors.

Parking is plentiful at most malls and is free for at least the first three hours. Street parking spaces can be hard to find but cost just Dhs.2 for one hour. You can pay in cash or with a Nol card at ticket machines, or those with a local SIM (p.48) can pay via SMS. Instructions are posted on ticket machines.

Taxi

Although the Metro is nearly fully operational, taxis remain a common way of getting around. There are seven companies operating nearly 8,000 metered cabs with a fixed fare structure. All cars are clean and modern, and the fares are cheaper than in most international cities. A fleet of 'ladies'

Essentials

SIGNATURE
PENTHOUSES

taxis,' with distinctive pink roofs and female drivers, are meant for female passengers and families only. The minimum fare is currently Dhs.10 and the pickup charge from the airport is Dhs.25. It is also possible to hire a taxi for 12 or 24 hour periods. Taxis can be flagged down by the side of the road, or you can order one through Dubai Transport by calling 04 208 0808. This number is also useful for complaints and lost item enquiries, both of which are usually dealt with promptly.

Unlike some other cities, there's no 'knowledge' style exam for cabbies here, so it helps to carry a map or the phone number of your destination in case you hail a driver who's new to the city.

Walking

Most cities in the UAE are very car-oriented and not designed to encourage walking. Additionally, summer temperatures of more than 45°C are not conducive to a leisurely stroll. The winter months, however, make walking a pleasant way to explore. There aren't many pavements however, so you're best heading to places such as 2nd Of December Road, Dubai Creek (p.92) and Jumeira Road (p.112) for a wander. There's also a running track along Jumeirah Open Beach (p.114), starting from Dubai

Street Strife

To make navigation more confusing, places may not always be referred to by their official name. For example, Jumeira Road is often known as Beach Road, and Interchange 1 on Sheikh Zayed Road is often called Defence Roundabout.

Marine Resort (dxbmarine.com), which is popular during the cooler months. Bucking the current trend, Downtown Dubai (p.98) and Dubai Marina are attractive communities designed with pedestrians in mind. Both are interesting places to walk around with plenty of cafes and shops to tempt you off the street.

Water Bus

Crossing the creek by a traditional abra is a common method of transport for many people living in Bur Dubai and Deira; for visitors, it's a must-do experience while in town. Abra stations have been upgraded recently, but the fares are still just Dhs.1.

Another recent addition to the creek was a fleet of air-conditioned water buses. These operate on four different routes crossing the creek, with fares set at Dhs.2 per one way trip. A 'tourist' route also operates, with a 45 minute creek tour costing around Dhs.25 per person.

It's also possible to take a scenic cruise on RTA's new Dubai Ferry; the modern ferries whisk you on a scenic ride and the routes depart from Dubai Marina and Al Ghubaiba (rta.ae).

Further Out

If you want to explore the UAE during your stay then you'll need a driver or rental car. The East Coast (p.136) is known for its wonderful coastline and watersports, all easily accessible within a two-hour drive. There is also a bus service to Abu Dhabi which runs hourly from Al Ghubaiba bus station. The journey takes two hours and costs Dhs.20. Contact the RTA on 800 9090 for more info.

Places To Stay

Nowhere does five-star like Dubai, but while there's a vast array of luxury options to choose from there's also something to suit every budget.

In addition to a high number of plush hotels, Dubai has plenty of four, three, two and one-star places, self-catering villas, hotel apartments and even a youth hostel. Furthermore, a new hotel seems to spring up every few months, so you're never short of choice when it comes to deciding where to rest your head.

Most hotels are within 30 minutes of the airport and tend to be either on the beach, by the creek or on Sheikh Zayed Road. The coastal options will probably allow access to a private beach, but if you're in Dubai on business then proximity to the financial and business areas of DIFC and Trade Centre is likely to be a priority. If you are in town to shop then take your pick as malls are everywhere – some with their own hotel. If you're here for a few days, why not combine your city stay with a night at a desert resort, such as Bab Al Shams (p.78)?

Popular hotels tend to get fully booked up in the high season, but big discounts and attractive packages are offered to summer visitors when temperatures in Dubai soar.

The VIP Set

With Roberto Cavalli's Cavalli Club (cavalliclub.com) at the Fairmont and an Armani Hotel at Burj Khalifa (armanihotels.com), there are plenty of places to show off your designer threads.

Dubai Marina

The Address Downtown Dubai

theaddress.com

04 436 8888

This luxury hotel has a range of excellent restaurants and one of the coolest bars in the city, Neos (p.313). It has two sister hotels at The Dubai Mall (04 438 8888) and Dubai Marina (04 436 7777).

Map 2 B3 **Metro** Burj Khalifa/Dubai Mall

Image Courtesy of Emaar Properties

Armani Hotel Dubai

dubai.armanihotels.com

04 888 3888

Oozing style and extravagance, the Armani Hotel occupies six floors of the Burj Khalifa and has 160 exquisite rooms and suites. There are four restaurants, an opulent bar and a chic spa.

Map 2 B2 **Metro** Burj Khalifa/Dubai Mall

Ascott Park Place Dubai

the-ascott.com

04 310 8555

Located along the bustling Sheikh Zayed Road, Ascott's luxuriously kitted serviced apartments of various sizes are available for short or longer stays. The facilities include a 40 metre swimming pool and a gym.

Map 2 E1 **Metro** World Trade Centre

Atlantis The Palm

atlantisthepalm.com
04 426 0000
Situated on the crescent of Palm Jumeirah, the sugary pink Atlantis offers 1,539 rooms including The Lost Chambers Suites which feature floor-to-ceiling windows looking into the aquarium.
Map 1 D1 **Metro** Nakheel

Burj Al Arab

jumeirah.com
04 301 7777
Architecturally unique, one of the world's tallest hotels stands 321 metres high on a man-made island, and is dramatic, lavish and exclusive. Guests are looked after by a host of butlers. Reservations are essential for dining.
Map 3 E1 **Metro** Mall Of The Emirates

Dubai Festival City

ichotelsgroup.com
DFC has two hotels to choose from. The InterContinental (04 701 1111) has extensive spa facilities and great views from all of its rooms and suites; next door is the five-star Crowne Plaza (04 701 2222) with the popular Belgian Beer Cafe (p.305).
Map 1 J4 **Metro** Emirates

Grosvenor House

grosvenorhouse-dubai.com
04 399 8888
This popular hotel in Dubai Marina features luxurious guest rooms and serviced apartments, as well as some iconic nightlife venues including Buddha Bar (p.306) and Gary Rhodes' Mezzanine (p.285).
Map 3 B1 **Metro** Dubai Marina

Hilton Dubai Jumeirah Resort

hilton.com
04 399 1111
Situated on a private stretch of sand a stone's throw from The Walk (p.105), this resort boasts good watersports facilities and popular eateries such as BiCE and The Wavebreaker beach bar (p.319).
Map 3 A1 **Metro** Jumeirah Lakes Towers

Jumeirah Beach Hotel

jumeirah.com
04 348 0000
One of Dubai's key landmarks. Built in the shape of a wave with a colourful interior, the hotel has 598 rooms, all with a sea view. It has several bars and restaurants, including Villa Beach (p.296) and 360° (p.302).
Map 3 E1 **Metro** Mall Of The Emirates

Le Royal Meridien Beach Resort & Spa

leroyalmeridien-dubai.com
04 399 5555
Set in landscaped gardens, this resort has a lush pool area and private beach, as well as excellent leisure facilities and a decent selection of bars and restaurants.
Map 3 B1 **Metro** Dubai Marina

Madinat Jumeirah

jumeirah.com
04 366 8888
This resort has two hotels, Al Qasr and Mina A'Salam, with 940 luxurious rooms and suites, and exclusive summer houses, all linked by man-made waterways. Between the hotels is Souk Madinat Jumeirah (p.120).
Map 3 E1 **Metro** Mall Of The Emirates

One&Only Royal Mirage

oneandonlyresorts.com
04 399 9999
Blessed with an intimate atmosphere, this hotel features unparalleled service and dining, while a luxury spa treatment here is pure indulgence. Try Moroccan cuisine at Tagine (p.292), or enjoy late nights at Kasbar.
Map 3 C1 **Metro** Nakheel

The Palace Downtown Dubai
theaddress.com
04 428 7888
Situated close to Burj Khalifa, The Palace boasts 242 deluxe rooms. There's butler service for all rooms, and views of the world's tallest building. Its Asado (p.252) steak restaurant is recommended.
Map 2 B3 **Metro** Burj Khalifa/Dubai Mall

Park Hyatt Dubai
dubai.park.hyatt.com
04 602 1234
Mediterranean and Moorish in style, the Park Hyatt has 225 rooms, each with a balcony or terrace with great views. It has a prime waterfront location next to Dubai Creek Golf & Yacht Club (p.152).
Map 4 D5 **Metro** GGICO

Pullman Dubai Mall Of The Emirates
pullman-dubai.com
04 377 2000
Located right next to the MoE, this plush hotel is a dream spot for keen shoppers. Also worth a mention is the roof terrace, which offers some of the best views in town.
Map 3 E2 **Metro** Mall Of The Emirates

Raffles Dubai
raffles.com
04 324 8888
Raffles has 248 guest rooms and suites and the Raffles Spa Dubai with a unique rooftop garden: an oasis of exotic flowers around a pool. There are nine restaurants and bars; The Noble House is a popular nightspot.
Map 4 B5 **Metro** Healthcare City

The Ritz-Carlton, Dubai
ritzcarlton.com
04 399 4000
Set right on the JBR beach (p.104), The Ritz-Carlton may stand low in comparison to the Marina towers but it excels in terms of style and service. Afternoon tea in the lobby is a must (p.274).
Map 3 A1 **Metro** Dubai Marina

The Westin Dubai Mina Seyahi Beach Resort & Marina
westinminaseyahi.com
04 399 4141
The Westin offers all the luxury amenities you would expect of a five-star hotel – in addition to popular evening venues and 1,200 metres of private beach close to Dubai Marina.
Map 3 B1 **Metro** Nakheel

Other Hotels

Downtown

With easy access to Dubai's financial centre and tourist attractions such as The Dubai Mall and Burj Khalifa, the Sheikh Zayed Road and Downtown hotels offer a balance of work and play. The glamorous Fairmont Dubai (04 332 5555, fairmont.com) sits opposite the city's financial hub and is home to some excellent dining options as well as Roberto Cavalli's signature nightspot, Cavalli Club (p.308). Nearby, the deluxe Shangri-La (04 343 8888, shangri-la.com) has a lovely pool area, as well as several popular bars and restaurants, including Amwaj (p.250), which is a contender for Dubai's best seafood joint. Located in the heart of Dubai's business district, the Ritz-Carlton Dubai International Financial Centre (04 372 2222, ritzcarlton.com) is a good bet for business trips; it's just steps away from DIFC and has good restaurants and a classy spa. Also in the DIFC area is Jumeirah Emirates Towers (04 330 0000, jumeirah.com), one of Dubai's most established luxury hotels. The nearby Dusit Thani (04 343 3333, dusit.com) lives up to its Thai ownership, housing the excellent far-eastern restaurant Benjarong.

Ski Stays

For the ultimate Dubai experience, check into Kempinski Hotel Mall Of The Emirates (kempinski-dubai. com); located in the world's busiest mall, the hotel's exclusive chalet rooms boast views of the snowy slopes of Ski Dubai (p.156).

Downtown vistas

Dubai Marina

With sea views, swimming pools and private beaches, sun worshippers are spoilt for choice in Dubai Marina and JBR (p.104). The Habtoor Grand Resort & Spa (04 399 5000, habtoorhotels.com) is another good option right on the beach. The Address Dubai Marina (04 436 7777, theaddress.com), meanwhile, boasts easy access to Dubai Marina Mall (p.203). The Dubai Marriott Harbour Hotel & Suites (04 319 4000, marriott.com) has spacious suites, each with its own kitchen and well-stocked bathroom. Nuran Serviced Residences (04 423 8877, nuran.com) is also a good choice if apartment hotel convenience in the vicinity of the beach is what you're after; the well-equipped apartments boast stunning marina views and the complex is conveniently located between Dubai Marina Yacht Club (dubaimarinayachtclub.com) and Dubai Marina Mall.

The Palm

In addition to Atlantis The Palm (p.69), the sandy shores of The Palm (p.118) are now home to other luxurious resorts, including the lavish Jumeirah Zabeel Saray (04 453 0000, jumeirah.com) and One&Only The Palm (04 440 1010, oneandonlyresorts.com).

On The Creek

The creekside hotels are ideally located for soaking up the atmosphere of old Dubai. Most of the rooms at the Sheraton Dubai Creek Hotel & Towers (04 228 1111, sheratondubaicreek. com) boast stunning views. Nearby, the Hilton

Dubai Creek (04 227 1111, hilton.com) houses some great restaurants – including Glasshouse Brasserie (p.268). The five-star Radisson Blu Hotel, Dubai Deira Creek (04 222 7171, radissonblu.com/hotel-dubaideiracreek) has a scenic pool and a host of popular dining options; Fish Market (p.266) is particularly recommended.

Near The Airport

Le Meridien Dubai (04 217 0000, lemeridien-dubai.com) offers easy access to the airport and the resort is home to some of the city's favourite restaurants, including the Meridien Village Terrace and Yalumba (p.299). The Al Bustan Rotana (04 282 0000, rotana.com) is another alternative in and around this residential neighbourhood.

Guesthouses & Hostels

The pick of the guesthouses are Fusion (fusionhotels. com/bedandbreakfastsindubai.html) and the XVA Art Hotel (xvagallery.com). The former features good facilities, including swimming pools, while the latter is nestled in a unique location in the heart of Bastakiya (p.86), one of the oldest heritage sites in the region. XVA Art Hotel's seven guestrooms ooze rustic charm and the adjacent gallery hosts interesting art exhibitions.

Dubai Youth Hostel (04 298 8161, uaeyha.com) offers single, double, triple and dorm rooms starting from Dhs.90.

Villas are another option for short or longer stays; visit mydubaistay.com for accommodation in different areas, with online availability, booking and a cost comparison chart.

Out Of The City

Al Maha, A Luxury Collection
Desert Resort & Spa

04 832 9900

al-maha.com

Dubai-Al Ain Rd

Set in 225 square kilometres of desert, the Al Maha resort, accessible only by a 4WD vehicle driven by your own field guide, is congruously set on the slopes of a rising dune and styled as a Bedouin camp. Wild Arabian oryx (maha) wander the resort, and each guest room is a stand-alone property, designed to resemble a traditional Bedouin tent. The suites feature a private terrace and infinity plunge pool. You can opt to dine in private on your patio or at the Al Diwaan restaurant; the choice is varied and there is a great wine list. The Saray Spa offers the full range of pampering and there are several activities you can take part in: one of the most popular is a sunset camel ride and champagne toast on the dunes.
Map 1 G7

Bab Al Shams Desert Resort & Spa

04 809 6100

themeydan.com

Nr Endurance Village, Bawadi

Like a desert mirage come to life, Bab Al Shams is a Bedouin fantasy escape. On approach, bamboo torches guide you to the low-rise building that blends into the imposing dunes that surround it, and the rooms have been designed to evoke a feeling of Bedouin living. Camel rides on the sand dunes are offered to guests, or you can chill out in one of the outdoor holistic swimming pools. Take the pampering up a notch by heading to the Satori Spa and, as the evening sets in, Al Sarab

Rooftop Lounge offers shisha and drinks. The Al Hadheerah restaurant offers a full-on Arabian experience, including a huge buffet, belly dancing and traditional music. **Map** 1 D7

Jebel Ali Golf Resort

04 814 5555
Nr Palm Jebel Ali, Waterfront · jaresortshotels.com
Just far enough out of Dubai to escape the hustle and bustle, this resort offers luxurious stays in resplendent surroundings, with a peaceful atmosphere. Set within 128 acres of lush, landscaped gardens, the recently renovated resort boasts an 800 metre private beach, a marina and a golf course. Guests can also enjoy horse riding, shooting and a variety of watersports. **Map** 1 A2

Exploring

Explore Dubai

From slick city attractions to expansive deserts, Dubai is an emirate of superlatives that will impress even the most seasoned traveller.

Dubai provides a wealth of contrasting images: Ferraris parked outside falafel shops, massive skyscrapers shading pristine mosques, billionaires, cranes, camels, palaces and windtowers. The city is filled with luxurious five-star hotels and huge shopping malls, it has some of the top nightspots in the Middle East, and is home to a range of museums, heritage sites and places of cultural interest. Quite a mix.

Don't let the traffic and ever-expanding footprint disorientate you – Dubai itself is fairly easy to navigate and explore, especially with the introduction of the Metro (p.56). The city runs along the Arabian Gulf coast, and the older sections of the city, such as Deira and Bur Dubai, are situated in the northern end and around the Dubai Creek. From there, the city stretches south along Sheikh Zayed Road towards new developments such as The Palm (p.118) and Dubai Marina (p.104).

Most of the city's historical attractions are located around the creek which, until recently, was the residential and commercial hub of the city. Bastakiya (p.86) and the souks of Deira (p.92) have managed to retain much of the old Dubai character and multiculturalism, with narrow streets selling everything from wholesale grain to traditional Emirati dress.

The bright lights of Deira

These are also the best areas to find a traditional Indian or Arabic meal. Try Saravana Bhavan (p.288) for a spicy south-Indian thali, or Bastakiah Nights (p.256) for a taste of Emirati machboos. If large and luxurious better describes the Dubai of your dreams, newer areas like Downtown Dubai (p.98), home to the world's tallest building, and Dubai Marina (p.104) should be your target destinations. The towering skyscrapers and enormous malls that fill these impressive developments contain some of the best shopping and nightlife in the Middle East. The Dubai Mall (p.204) houses some 1,200 shops, while the sheer volume of restaurants and bars on the Al Sufouh strip (p.118), The Palm and the Marina could easily keep you occupied for years.

Heritage Sites

Museums & Art Galleries

Parks

Beaches & Beach Parks

Bastakiya: Old Dubai

For heritage and a glimpse into Dubai's past, Bastakiya's narrow streets are not to be missed.

If you're in search of a dose of tradition, step out of the modern world and into a pocket of the city that harks back to a bygone era. The Bastakiya area is one of the oldest heritage sites in Dubai and certainly the most atmospheric. The neighbourhood dates from the early 1900s when traders from the Bastak area of southern Iran were encouraged to settle there by tax concessions granted by Sheikh Maktoum bin Hashar, the ruler of Dubai at the time.

The area is characterised by traditional windtower houses, built around courtyards and clustered together along a winding maze of alleyways. The distinctive four-sided windtowers (barjeel), seen on top of the traditional flat-roofed buildings, were an early form of air conditioning.

There are some excellent cultural establishments in and around Bastakiya, and a short stroll along the creek will bring you to the Textile Souk and abra station, from where you can cross the water to explore the souks on the Deira side (see p.95). You can make a single crossing on a communal abra for Dhs.1, or hire your own (plus driver) for an hour-long tour for Dhs.100.

Dubai Museum

Al Fahidi Fort, Al Souk Al Kabeer

04 353 1862

definitelydubai.com

Located in and under Al Fahidi Fort, which dates back to 1787, this museum is creative and well thought-out. All parts of life from Dubai's past are represented in an attractive and interesting way; walk through a souk from the 1950s, stroll through an oasis, see into a traditional house, get up close to local wildlife, learn about the archaeological finds or go 'underwater' to discover the pearl diving and fishing industries. There are some entertaining mannequins to pose with too. Entry costs Dhs.3 for adults and Dhs.1 for children under 6 years old. Open daily 08:30 to 20:30 (14:00 to 19:00 on Fridays). **Map** 4 C2 **Metro** Al Fahidi

Heritage & Diving Village

Nr Sheikh Saeed House,
Al Shindagha

04 393 7139

definitelydubai.com

Located near the mouth of Dubai Creek, the Heritage & Diving Village focuses on Dubai's maritime past, pearl diving traditions and architecture. Visitors can observe traditional potters and weavers practising their craft the way it has been done for centuries. Local women serve traditionally cooked snacks – one of the rare opportunities you'll have to sample genuine Emirati cuisine. Camel rides are also available most afternoons and evenings. The Village is particularly lively during the Dubai Shopping Festival (p.53) and Eid celebrations, with performances including traditional sword dancing. Open daily 08:30 to 22:00 (Fridays 15:30 to 22:00). **Map** 4 C1 **Metro** Al Ghubaiba

The Majlis Gallery

04 353 6233

Bastakiya, Al Souk Al Kabeer — themajlisgallery.com

The Majlis Gallery is a converted Arabian house, complete with windtowers and courtyard. Small, whitewashed rooms lead off the central garden and host exhibitions by contemporary artists. In addition to the fine art collection, there's an extensive range of hand-made glass, pottery, fabrics, frames and unusual furniture. The gallery hosts exhibitions throughout the year, and is worth visiting at any time. Open Saturday to Thursday, 10:00 to 18:00.
Map 4 C2 **Metro** Al Fahidi

Sheikh Mohammed Centre For Cultural Understanding

04 353 6666

Bastakiya, Al Souk Al Kabeer — cultures.ae

This facility was established to help visitors and residents understand the customs and traditions of the UAE. It organises tours in Jumeirah Mosque (p.113), a walking tour of the Bastakiya area, as well as cultural breakfasts and lunches. The centre is worth a look for the majlis-style rooms around the courtyard and great views through the palm trees and windtowers. Open Sunday to Thursday 08:00 to 18:00 and Saturday 09:00 to 13:00. **Map** 4 C2 **Metro** Al Fahidi

Sheikh Saeed Al Maktoum House

04 393 7139

Nr Heritage & Diving Village, Al Shindagha

Dating from 1896, this carefully restored house-turned-museum is built in the traditional manner of the Gulf coast, using coral covered in lime and sand-coloured plaster. The

Heritage & Diving Village

interesting displays in many rooms show rare and wonderful photographs of life in Dubai pre-oil. Entry is Dhs.2 for adults, Dhs.1 for children and free for children under 6 years old.
Map 4 C1 **Metro** Al Ghubaiba

XVA Gallery

04 353 5383

Bastakiya, Al Souk Al Kabeer · xvagallery.com

Situated in the centre of Bastakiya, this is one of Dubai's most interesting art galleries. Originally a windtower house, it's worth a visit for its architecture alone. The gallery hosts exhibitions throughout the year and there's also a boutique hotel with guest rooms offering views over the minarets to Bur Dubai. Open Saturday to Thursday, 09:00 to 19:00.
Map 4 C2 **Metro** Al Fahidi

If you only do one thing in...
Bastakiya

Get schooled at the informative Dubai Museum (p.87). Learn about life in Dubai 50 years ago to really appreciate how much has changed.

Best for...

Eating & Drinking: For an atmospheric evening of Arabian food in a traditional setting, book a table at Bastakiah Nights (p.256).

Families: Let the kids hop on a camel while you gorge on freshly baked bread, all in the middle of living history at the Heritage & Diving Village (p.87).

Relaxation: Duck into tranquillity at The Majlis Gallery (p.88) or XVA (p.89).

Shopping: A visit to the Textile Souk (p.199) is a memorable affair, and if your haggling skills are up to par you could take home a pashmina at a bargain price.

Sightseeing: The winding alleyways of Bastakiya (p.86) will linger in the memory long after you leave Dubai.

Traditional Arabian architecture

Deira & The Creek: Dubai's Port

Deira's busy streets capture the bustling essence of old Dubai, while the emirate's trading traditions live on at the creek.

Once the residential hub of Dubai, Deira remains an incredibly atmospheric area. Narrow convoluted streets bustle with activity while gold, spices, perfumes and general goods are touted in its numerous souks. Likewise, Dubai Creek, upon which Deira sits, was once the centre of Dubai commerce. Both sides of the creek are lined by corniches that come alive in the evenings as residents head out for a stroll and traders take stock. Take the time to meander along the Deira side of the creek where men in traditional south-Asian garb unload wooden dhows that are docked by the water's edge and tightly packed with everything from fruit and vegetables to televisions and maybe even a car or two. And no visitor should leave without experiencing a trip across the water on a commuter abra (p.65) for Dhs.1, or a tourist abra (Dhs.100 for an hour's private trip).

Start with a wander through the Textile Souk (p.199) on the Bur Dubai side before taking an abra towards Deira. Once on the Deira side, cross the corniche and head towards the souk district. First stop is the Spice Souk (p.198), where the aroma of saffron and cumin fills the air. Nearby, the streets in and around the Gold Souk (p.194) are filled with shops shimmering with gold and platinum. If it's exotic rugs you're after, then Deira Tower on Al Nasr Square (Map 4 D2) is worth a visit. Around 40 shops offer a colourful profusion of carpets

Clocktower Roundabout

from Iran, Pakistan, Turkey and Afghanistan to suit everyone's taste and pocket. For dinner with a view, head to the top of the Hyatt Regency where Al Dawaar (p.247) hosts an incredible buffet within its rotating dining room. Afterwards, go for a stroll along the Gulf side of Deira corniche. If you're staying on the Deira side of town, Al Mamzar has a great section of beach (see below).

Al Ahmadiya School & Heritage House   04 226 0286
Nr Dubai Public Libraries, Al Khor St, Al Ras

Established in 1912 for Dubai's elite, Al Ahmadiya School was the earliest regular school in the city. A visit here is an excellent opportunity to see the history of education in the UAE. Situated in what is becoming a small centre for heritage (Al Souk Al Kabeer), it is an interesting example of a traditional Emirati family home, and dates back to 1890. Admission to both is free. Open Saturday to Thursday 08:30 to 20:30 and 14:00 to 20:30 on Friday. **Map** 4 C1 **Metro** Al Ras

Mamzar Beach Park   04 296 6201
Nr Hamriya Port, Al Mamzar   dm.gov.ae

With its four clean beaches, open spaces and plenty of greenery, Al Mamzar is a popular spot. The well-maintained beaches have sheltered areas for swimming and changing rooms with showers. Air-conditioned chalets, with barbecues, can be rented on a daily basis, costing from Dhs.160 to Dhs.210. There are two swimming pools with lifeguards on duty. Entrance is Dhs.5 per person or Dhs.30 per car (including all occupants). **Map** 1 K2 **Metro** Al Qiyadah

Creekside Souks

Al Ras

Deira's three main souks – the Spice Souk, the Fish Souk and the Gold Souk – present some of the best examples of living heritage that Dubai has to offer. Smelly as it may be, an early morning trip through the Fish Souk makes for a great photo opportunity. The Gold Souk (p.194) gets crowded on weekend afternoons, but spend an hour or two here during the week and enjoy a form of window shopping that's very different from a mall experience. For the best insight into the region's varied cuisines, take a walk through the Spice Souk where you'll be bombarded by the colours and smells of spices you've never heard of. Just across the creek on the Bur Dubai side sits the covered Textile Souk (p.199) with its myriad of bright fabrics. An abra ride across the creek is a must while in this part of town. **Map** 4 C2 **Metro** Al Ras

Dubai Dolphinarium

Creek Park, Umm Hurair 2

04 336 9773
dubaidolphinarium.ae

Located within the Creek Park, the main attraction here is the popular seal and dolphin show which runs twice a day during the week and three times daily at the weekends (closed on Sundays). During the show you will get to admire the resident bottlenose dolphins and, afterwards, you can get your picture taken with these adorable creatures. Prices start from Dhs.120 for adults and Dhs.80 for children; check the website for details of family discounts and other options – including an opportunity to swim with the dolphins in one of the pools. **Map** 4 C5 **Metro** Dubai Healthcare City

If you only do one thing in...
Deira & The Creek

Watch the dhows unload at the corniche, then head for a stroll around Dubai's famous souks.

Best for...

Eating & Drinking: Hop on a dhow for a delicious dinner cruise (p.227). This is by far the best way to get your fill of food, facts and photographs.

Families: Give the kids an experience of a lifetime at the Dubai Dolphinarium (p.95).

Relaxation: Step into the calm courtyard of the Al Ahmadiya School & Heritage House (p.94), where you'll find some quiet in the Deira storm.

Shopping: Stroll through the glittering streets of the Gold Souk (p.194) before following your nose to the Spice Souk (p.198).

Sightseeing: Reserve a table at the Hyatt Regency's Al Dawaar (p.247). The city's only revolving restaurant offers fantastic views of the creek and beyond.

Clockwise from top: an abra on Dubai Creek, Spice Souk, a dhow close-up

Downtown & Sheikh Zayed Road

The world's tallest building, Dubai's largest mall and the most photographed skyline in the city are all in Dubai's glitziest area.

Among the newest places in town to explore, Downtown Dubai is a spectacular mix of shops, restaurants, entertainment and architecture, while nearby is a stretch of Dubai's original stunning skyscraper strip, which lines either side of Sheikh Zayed Road and features some of the city's top hotels and building design. At the heart of Downtown Dubai is the shimmering Burj Khalifa; the world's tallest tower points like a needle more than 800m skywards and counts an Armani hotel (p.68), scenic spot At The Top (p.21) and the world's highest restaurant, At.mosphere (p.253), among its attractions. By its base are The Dubai Mall (p.204), Old Town, and The Dubai Fountain (p.100).

   The Dubai Mall is a huge shopping centre full of top-end retail brands, excellent eateries and some fantastic entertainment options, such as Dubai Aquarium and SEGA Republic. There are two The Address hotels in the area, with the views from the 63rd floor Neos bar (p.313) at The Address Downtown Dubai well worth taking in. Old Town, which is home to the atmospheric Souk Al Bahar (p.197), takes strong influences from traditional Arabia with its mosaics, passageways and fortress-like finishes, all of which are beautifully lit at night. Other hotels in the Downtown area include The Palace Hotel and Al Manzil, which are home to Asado steakhouse (p.252) and upmarket sports bar Nezesaussi (p.314) respectively.

The buzzing strip over on Sheikh Zayed Road is known for the striking architecture of its high-rise residential buildings, office towers and top-class hotels. From the Dubai World Trade Centre to Interchange 1 (known as Defence Roundabout), the wide, skyscraping 3.5km stretch is the subject of many a photo, as well as after-hours hook-ups in the various happening hotspots. With so many residents, tourists and business people around, this area really comes alive at night, as the crowds flit from restaurants to bars to clubs in the area's many hotels (p.66).

Dubai Aquarium & Underwater Zoo   04 448 5200
The Dubai Mall,
  Downtown Dubai   thedubaiaquarium.com
The bewildering variety of tropical fish (over 33,000 in total) is displayed to passing shoppers free of charge. For a closer view of the main tank's inhabitants, which include fearsome looking but generally friendly sand tiger sharks, you can pay to walk through the 270° viewing tunnel. Also well worth a look is the Underwater Zoo, which has residents such as penguins, piranhas and an octopus. If you're feeling adventurous, you can even go for a scuba dive in the tank (call ahead to book). A ticket to the interactive Underwater Zoo and Tunnel Experience costs Dhs.55.
Map 2 C3 **Metro** Burj Khalifa/Dubai Mall

The Dubai Fountain

Nr Burj Khalifa, Downtown Dubai   thedubaimall.com

This spectacular Downtown centrepiece draws crowds to witness the regular evening shows. Designed by the same team that created the famous Bellagio fountains in Las Vegas, the water, light and music combination is a captivating showstopper. Jets of water shoot 150m into the air along the length of the Burj lake in synchronisation with classical and Arabic music, while the Burj Khalifa at night forms a memorable backdrop. The show takes place daily at 13:00 and 13:30, and then every half hour from 18:00 until 23:00 (weekdays) or 23:30 (weekends). It can be viewed from outside The Dubai Mall and Souk Al Bahar, or you could grab a table at one of the many outdoor restaurants in this area.

Map 2 C3 **Metro** Burj Khalifa/Dubai Mall

Jumeirah Emirates Towers

Sheikh Zayed Rd, Trade Centre   04 330 0000
jumeirah.com

These twin towers are a true Dubai landmark. At 350m, the office tower was the tallest building in the Middle East and Europe until the Burj Khalifa surpassed it. The smaller tower, at 305m, houses the Emirates Towers hotel plus many eating and drinking spots. Harry Ghatto's is a city favourite for karaoke, while the Ivy (04 319 8767) offers fine fare. For a scenic thrill, the views from the aptly named 51st floor Vu's Bar (p.298) are superb. If shopping makes your heart beat, The Boulevard is probably Dubai's most exclusive mall.

Map 2 D2 **Metro** Emirates Towers

The Dubai Fountain & Old Town Island

SEGA Republic

04 448 8484

The Dubai Mall, Downtown Dubai · segarepublic.com

This indoor theme park located in The Dubai Mall offers a range of indoor thrills, courtesy of the nine main attractions and the 200 arcade games. A Power Pass (Dhs.140) gets you all-day access to the big attractions, which include stomach-flipping rides like the Sonic Hopper, the SpinGear and the Halfpipe Canyon. Unlike many other shopping mall amusement centres, SEGA Republic is for all ages, and features some truly unique thrills.

Map 2 C3 **Metro** Burj Khalifa/Dubai Mall

If you only do one thing in...

Downtown Dubai & Sheikh Zayed Road

Dine alfresco while watching the nightly Dubai Fountain shows (p.100).

Best for...

Eating & Drinking: Japanese restaurant Zuma in DIFC offers one of the best, funkiest, fine-dining experiences in Dubai (p.300).

Families: Take the kids to SEGA Republic (p.101) and be amazed at how far technology has come.

Relaxation: Take time out at The Spa at The Palace; after a treatment here you'll feel like royalty (04 428 7805).

Shopping: With over 1,000 stores, The Dubai Mall is a shopaholic's paradise (p.204).

Sightseeing: The sweeping views from the world's highest restaurant At.mosphere (p.253) can't be beaten.

Dubai Marina & JBR: New Dubai

Head to the Marina for high-rise heaven, a thriving cafe culture and bustling beach action.

Previously home to just a handful of waterfront hotels, the Marina is the epitome of the rise of 'New Dubai' to modern prominence. Apartment buildings (finished or still under construction) have sprouted up along every inch of the man-made waterway, while between the marina and the shore is the massive Jumeirah Beach Residence (JBR) development, which now dwarfs the five-star beach resorts such as the Hilton (p.70) and Ritz-Carlton (p.73). The walkways that run around the marina and parallel to the coast have evolved into lively strips of cafes and restaurants, which throng with people in the evenings when the lit-up skyscrapers are at their most impressive. On the water, luxury boats fill the marina's berths, and thrill seekers take to the sea to parasail or waterski.

JBR Beach
Dubai Marina

At nearly 2km long, this bay of golden sand is massively popular. The spaces in front of the hotels are reserved for guests, but there are plenty of areas in between that fill with families and groups of friends at weekends. The waters are fairly calm here and the shallow areas are scattered with bathers, while the hotels offer a variety of watersports such as parasailing that anyone can sign up for. There is a big carpark, but this gets fairly congested at peak times. **Map** 3 A1 **Metro** Dubai Marina

Marina Walk

Dubai Marina

The Marina Walk boulevard starts at the base of Dubai Marina Towers and provides an almost continuous pedestrian access around the 11km perimeter of the water. The promenade is home to several restaurants and cafes such as popular Lebanese restaurant and shisha spot Chandelier (04 366 3603). It is a great place for a stroll at any time but it really comes to life in the evenings and cooler months when you can sit and gaze out across the rows of yachts and the flashing lights of high-rise hotels and apartments. For speedier explorations, you'll find bicycle rental spots along the way. Also on the walk is the Dubai Marina Mall (p.203), and the Dubai Marina Yacht Club, which houses the popular Aquara restaurant and bar (p.251).

Map 3 A1 **Metro** Dubai Marina

The Walk, Jumeirah Beach Residence

Jumeirah Beach Residence, Dubai Marina

The Walk at JBR is an outdoor parade of shops, restaurants and hotels parallel to the beach and is a huge leisure-time draw for Dubai residents. Strolling from one end to the other of this 1.7km promenade will take you past a whole host of retail and eating options, with the scores of alfresco diners and Saturday strollers providing some excellent people-watching. From Wednesday to Saturday the outdoor Covent Garden Market by Rimal court is an added attraction, with street entertainers and craft stalls creating a colourful atmosphere (see p.193). **Map** 3 A1 **Metro** Dubai Marina

If you only do one thing in...
Dubai Marina & JBR

Head to the beach for a morning swim before treating yourself to an alfresco breakfast on The Walk.

Best for...

Eating & Drinking: Tuck into seafood alfresco at Dubai Marina Yacht Club's Aquara (p.251) and watch marina life sail by as you dine.

Families: Give the family the thrill of a lifetime with a camel ride on JBR Beach.

Relaxation: End your day on the beach by taking a leisurely stroll along the golden sands, then head out to Ritz-Carlton's opulent spa (p.175) for a spot of pampering.

Shopping: Wander through the Covent Garden Market (p.193) on The Walk and pick up some works by Dubai's emerging designers and artisans.

Sightseeing: Take the hour-long Captain Jack dhow tour (Bristol Middle East, p.145) for some spectacular views of the Marina and JBR from the water.

Waterside living in Dubai Marina

Festival City & Garhoud

Relaxed and refined, Festival City is an oasis of calm in an otherwise rushed, modern metropolis.

Situated on the creek just down from Deira, Festival City has grown into a massive eating, shopping and entertainment complex. With an open marina, a bowling centre and cinema, a world-class golf course and several restaurants, Festival City has enough attractions to warrant a day of exploring, strolling and window shopping.

Festival City is bounded at one end by Al Badia Golf Club (p.151) and its gorgeous clubhouse, and at the other by the InterContinental (p.69) and Crowne Plaza (p.69) hotel towers which house the Belgian Beer Café (p.305). In between sits the Festival Waterfront Centre, one of Dubai's more spacious and relaxed shopping malls, as well as an outdoor concert venue that has hosted Paul Weller, Kylie Minogue, Maroon 5 and Queen. A canal-like waterway, complete with tiny passenger boats and alfresco dining options, meanders through the area and is perfect for post-meal, evening strolls. For a truly authentic dining experience, look no further than Al Fanar (p.247), an atmospheric restaurant that specialises in Emirati cuisine. Aside from shopping and dining, Festival City hosts several events throughout the year, including dragonboat races, children's events and fashion shows. Check out festivalcentre.com for a schedule of upcoming events.

Nearby in Garhoud, the Irish Village (p.312) has long been

Festival City

an institution on the Dubai drinking scene with live music and several annual events such as the Dubai Sound City music festival. Next door, the Century Village is a collection of licensed alfresco restaurants including Sushi Sushi (04 282 9908) and St Tropez (04 286 9029). The Dubai Tennis Stadium is home of the Dubai Duty Free Tennis Championships (p.165), while The Aviation Club has good fitness and leisure facilities; a new hotel is also underway here. A bit closer to Deira is the Dubai Creek Golf & Yacht Club, incorporating the creekside Boardwalk restaurant (p.258) and Park Hyatt Dubai (p.72), home to the lovely Amara Spa (p.170) and The Thai Kitchen restaurant (p.293).

If you only do one thing in...

Festival City & Garhoud

Spend an evening over pints and live music at the Irish Village (p.312), one of the city's oldest and most popular pubs.

Best for...

Eating & Drinking: Tuck into regional specialities at Emirati restaurant Al Fanar (p.247).

Families: The bowling alley in Festival Waterfront Centre (p.108) is a blast for all ages.

Sightseeing: The views from Boardwalk (p.258) are some of the best in the city.

Shopping: The spacious, well-designed halls of Festival Waterfront Centre (p.108) offer a calmer shopping environment than the busier, larger malls.

Relaxation: Indulge yourself with a treatment at the highly rated Amara Spa at the Park Hyatt Dubai (p.72).

Jumeira: Beachside Life

Jumeira's beaches, boutiques and art galleries offer a pleasant retreat from the city's bustling core.

Jumeira might not have the exotic atmosphere or history of Deira, but its beaches, shopping centres and pleasant, wide roads make up for it. Head out here for a glimpse into the good life: Jumeira is one of the most desirable addresses for well-off expats and home to the infamous, coiffeured 'Jumeira Janes' – well-off expat women who can often be found in the boutiques along Jumeira Road and the shops in Mercato (p.208). The popular Jumeira Open Beach is open to all free of charge. There are showers and lifeguards, but unfortunately the beach also attracts a few voyeurs, so you may prefer to try the more private Jumeirah Beach Park (p.113). Just outside Jumeira, on the border with Satwa, lies 2nd Of December Road – the main destination for anyone needing to feed their post-club hunger, show off their expensive customised cars, or watch the city pass by as they enjoy some street-side Lebanese fare. If you're out past midnight, don't miss having a bite at either Al Mallah (p.248) or Ravi's (p.284). That's not to say it doesn't have any culture; Jumeirah Mosque (p.113) is one of the most recognisable places of worship in the city and welcomes tourists with tours and educational programmes, while the many galleries will keep art enthusiasts happy.

Dubai International Art Centre

04 344 4398

Villa 27, Street 75b, Jumeira 1

artdubai.com

Since its founding in 1976, Dubai International Art Centre has been a hub for all things artsy in Jumeira. In addition to nurturing local talent by organising training and workshops, the premises also house Gallery 76. This exhibition venue has been hosting interesting displays of art by local and international artists alike since 2005; the exhibitions range from paintings, sculpture and photography to outdoors installations. **Map** 1 G2 **Metro** Business Bay

Jumeirah Beach Park

04 349 2555

Nr Jumeirah Beach Club, Jumeira Rd, Jumeira 2

dm.gov.ae

You get the best of both worlds here with plenty of grassy areas and vast expanses of beach. The facilities include sunlounger and parasol hire, lifeguards, toilets, showers, snack bar, play park and barbecue pits. Entry is Dhs.5 per person or Dhs.20 per car, including all occupants. Mondays are for women and children only. Open daily from 07:00, closing at 23:00 Sunday to Wednesday, and at 23:30 Thursday to Saturday and on holidays. **Map** 1 G2 **Metro** Business Bay

Jumeirah Mosque

04 353 6666

Jumeira Rd, Jumeira 1

cultures.ae

This is the most beautiful mosque in the city and perhaps the best known. Non-Muslims are not usually permitted entry to a mosque, but the Sheikh Mohammed Centre for Cultural Understanding (p.88) organises weekly tours (Saturday,

Sunday, Tuesday and Thursday mornings at 10:00). Visitors are guided around the mosque and told all about the building, and then the hosts give a talk on Islam and the prayer ritual. You must dress conservatively – no shorts and no sleeveless tops. Women must also cover their hair with a head scarf or shawl, and all visitors will be asked to remove their shoes. Cameras are allowed and large groups can book private tours.

Map 1 H2 **Metro** World Trade Centre

Jumeirah Open Beach

Nr Dubai Marine Beach Resort & Spa, Jumeira 1

One of the most popular free beaches in the city, this clean area offers both showers and lifeguards. Unfortunately, men staring at the sunbathing women can often be found loitering in the area. They may make the scene uncomfortable, but on the whole they mean no harm. A sprung running and bike track runs the length of the beach.

Map 1 H2 **Metro** Emirates Towers

Majlis Ghorfat Um Al Sheif

Jumeira Rd, Jumeira 3

04 852 1374

definitelydubai.com

Constructed in 1955 from coral stone and gypsum, this simple building was used by the late Sheikh Rashid bin Saeed Al Maktoum as a summer residence. The ground floor is an open veranda, while upstairs the majlis (meeting place) is decorated with carpets, cushions, lanterns and rifles. The Majlis is located just off Jumeira Road on Street 17, beside HSBC bank. Entry is Dhs.1 for adults and free for children

Jumeira Mosque

under 6 years old. It opens at 08:30 and closes at 20:30 every day except Friday, when it opens at 14:30.

Map 1 F2 **Metro** Business Bay

Safa Park

04 349 2111

Nr Union Co-op & Choithram, Al Wasl

dm.gov.ae

This huge, artistically divided park is a great place to escape the commotion of nearby Sheikh Zayed Road. Its many sports fields, barbecue sites and play areas make it one of the few places where locals and expats come together. There's a large boating lake in the centre of the park, tennis and basketball courts for the public and a flea market held on the first Saturday of every month. There is also a permanent ladies' garden within the park. Entry costs Dhs.3 (free for children under 3 years old). There's a great running track around the park's perimeter.

Map 1 G2 **Metro** Business Bay

If you only do one thing in...
Jumeira

Take a tour of the most beautiful mosque in the city (p.112), and one of the few in the country open to non-Muslims.

Best for...

Eating & Drinking: Dine on fantastic Cuban fare while listening to a live Latino band at El Malecon (p.263).

Families: Head to Jumeirah Beach Park (p.113), rent a sunbed and parasol, and experience the Dubai you've seen in the brochures.

Relaxation: Feel like a 'Jumeira Jane' by slipping into Elche for a treatment (04 349 4942).

Shopping: Enjoy a wander through the malls and thriving independent fashion boutiques that line Jumeira Road.

Sightseeing: Spend an afternoon at Jumeirah Beach Park (p.113) and watch the Burj Al Arab from afar.

Clockwise from top: Jumeira Beach Park, Majlis Ghorfat Um Al Sheef, Mercato

The Palm Jumeirah & Al Sufouh

With a modern man-made wonder, world-famous hotels, sandy shores and an indoor ski slope, this area is a must for any itinerary.

This stretch of coastline, between Dubai Marina and Umm Suqeim, is home to some of the most prestigious and popular resorts in Dubai. From the exclusive, iconic Burj Al Arab and Jumeirah Beach Hotel at one end, along Al Sufouh Road past the One&Only Royal Mirage, The Westin and, finally, at the other end, Le Meridien Mina Seyahi (with everyone's favourite beach party bar, Barasti), this section of the Gulf contains more pricey hotels than a Monopoly set. In the middle of all this, stretching several kilometres out to sea, is The Palm, Dubai's original mind-boggling man-made island, with its countless luxury villas and apartments, and the Disney-esque Atlantis hotel as its crowning showpiece. Within these resorts are dozens of excellent eating and drinking choices, open to all, while Souk Madinat Jumeirah (p.120) and, nearby in Al Barsha, Mall Of The Emirates (p.207) are both great spots for shopping, dining and all-round entertainment.

Sun and water lovers are well catered for here too, with two waterparks (Wild Wadi and Aquaventure), a great public beach and several full-service private hotel beaches available for day use. If the beautiful weather gets to be too much, there's always Ski Dubai (p.156) where you can have a jaunt in the snow to cool you down.

Atlantis The Palm

04 426 0000
Crescent Rd, Palm Jumeirah   atlantisthepalm.com

As the name suggests, the water theme is an important part of the Atlantis set-up. Aquaventure is the resort's thrilling water park; get the adrenaline pumping by making the Leap of Faith, a 27.5 metre near-vertical drop, or take the various slides that shoot you through a series of tunnels surrounded by shark-infested waters. Alternatively, The Rapids will carry you around a 2.3 kilometre river, complete with waterfalls and wave surges. Another attraction here is Dolphin Bay, where you can get close up in the water with playful bottlenose dolphins, while inside the hotel is the Lost Chambers aquarium, which contains 65,000 colourful inhabitants. The hotel is also home to several top restaurants, including Nobu (p.280) and Rostang (p.286). **Map** 1 C1 **Metro** Nakheel

Burj Al Arab

04 301 7777
Nr Wild Wadi, Jumeira Rd, Umm Suqeim   jumeirah.com

The Burj Al Arab is one of the most photographed sights in Dubai. The billowing-sail structure is a stunning piece of architecture – and inside it's no less spectacular. If your budget allows, you shouldn't miss the opportunity to sample luxury at the spa, bars and restaurants. Particularly recommended is afternoon tea at Sahn Eddar (p.288) or the Skyview Bar (p.316), and fine seafood dining at Al Mahara (p.248). Keep in mind that you won't be allowed into the Burj Al Arab unless you have a reservation at one of the dining venues. Advanced booking is required.

Map 3 E1 **Metro** Mall Of The Emirates

Souk Madinat Jumeirah

04 366 8888
jumeirah.com

Al Sufouh Rd, Al Sufouh 1

Souk Madinat Jumeirah is located just a stone's throw from the Burj Al Arab and next-door neighbour Al Qasr. Built to resemble a traditional Arabian market, the souk is a maze of alleyways featuring 95 open-fronted shops and boutiques where you can find everything from swimwear to souvenirs. For weary shoppers, there are numerous coffee shops and bars, as well as Talise (p.178), an outstanding spa. This is also a popular destination for dining, including Chinese fusion at Zheng He's (p.300). **Map** 3 E1 **Metro** Mall Of The Emirates

Wild Wadi Water Park

04 348 4444
jumeirah.com

Jumeira Rd, Umm Suqeim 3

Spread over 12 acres beside Jumeirah Beach Hotel, this water park has a host of aquatic rides and attractions to suit all ages and bravery levels. Depending on how busy it is, you may have to queue for some of the rides, but the wait is worth it. After paying the entrance fee, there is no limit to the number of times you can ride. The park opens at 10:00 and the closing time depends on the time of year. Admission is Dhs.220 for adults and Dhs.175 for children. Thursday is ladies' night for those girls who'd rather not show their skin to everyone. There is also a 'sundowner' rate (for the last two hours of opening), when adults pay Dhs.185 and children below 1.1 meters pay Dhs.145.
Map 3 E1 **Metro** Mall Of The Emirates

The Palm Jumeirah & Al Sufouh

If you only do one thing in...

The Palm Jumeirah & Al Sufouh

Take in the (recreated) old by wandering Souk Madinat Jumeirah's alleyways before heading to the beach for a view of the new in the form of the Burj Al Arab.

Best for...

Eating & Drinking: Sip with a view at Après (p.251) while watching people hurtle down Ski Dubai's slopes.

Families: Head to Atlantis' water attractions (p.119) to kick back on the lazy river, watch the dolphins or stretch out on the hotel's private beach.

Relaxation: Pamper yourself in the incredible luxury of Talise Spa (p.178) at Madinat Jumeirah.

Shopping: Mall Of The Emirates is a major 'New Dubai' dining and entertainment hub – and it also has some of the region's best shopping (p.207).

Sightseeing: Take a ride on The Palm's monorail, which provides great views of the coastline, plus the chance to nosey at some of the island's villas (p.118).

Clockwise from top: Al Mahara, Madinat Jumeirah, Dubai's icons

Umm Hurair: Creekside Adventure

Once known as the leisure capital of the city, people now flock to this area for luxury shopping, lazy afternoons and family fun.

Together, Oud Metha, Umm Hurair and Zabeel form a park-filled corner of Dubai that lines the bottom half of the creek. Wafi (p.212) and Lamcy Plaza are popular shopping spots both for bargains and international fashion labels, while the pyramid-shaped Raffles Dubai hotel (p.73) has several top-notch dining options.

Children's City
04 334 0808
Creek Park, Umm Hurair 2
childrencity.ae
Children's City offers kids hands-on educational amusement facilities. There's a planetarium, a nature centre, and the Discovery Space, revealing the miracles of the human body. It is aimed at 5 to 12 year olds, although toddlers and teenagers – or even adults – may also find it entertaining.
Map 4 C5 **Metro** Healthcare City

Creek Park
04 336 7633
Nr Al Maktoum & Al Garhoud Bridges
Umm Hurair 2
dm.gov.ae
Creek Park is blessed with acres of gardens, fishing piers, barbecue sites, children's play areas, restaurants and kiosks. Running along the park's 2.5km stretch of creek frontage is a

Zabeel Park

cable car system, allowing visitors an unrestricted view from 30m in the air. Entrance costs Dhs.5.

Map 4 C6 **Metro** Oud Metha

Zabeel Park

04 398 6888

Nr Trade Centre, Shk Khalifa
Bin Zayed Rd, Al Kifaf

dm.gov.ae

Providing an oasis of greenery in dusty Dubai, Zabeel Park has several recreational areas, a jogging track, a mini cricket pitch, a football field, a boating lake and an amphitheatre, plus a number of restaurants and cafes. Mondays are for ladies only. Entry costs Dhs.5 for anyone over 2 years old.

Map 4 A3 **Metro** Al Jafiliya

Exploring

MAKE UP FOR EVE

If you only do one thing in...
Umm Hurair

Sample the joys of shopping, spas and oversized cocktails all under one roof at Wafi (p.212).

Best for...

Eating & Drinking: There are plenty of top restaurants at Wafi, but the modern Indian cuisine of Asha's (p.253) truly captures the imagination.

Families: Let the kids loose at Children's City (p.124) – great fun for adults too.

Relaxation: Take a picnic to Creek Park (p.124) and watch the park and creek action unfold.

Shopping: Find unforgettable gifts at the underground souk of Khan Murjan (p.196).

Sightseeing: Squeeze into a cable car in Creek Park (p.124) for great views over the water.

Clockwise from top: Raffles, Wafi, Creek Park

Umm Hurair: Creekside Adventure

Off The Beaten Track

Some of Dubai's funkier cultural hotspots are found in some of the most unlikely places.

Outside of the areas already covered in this chapter, some sightseeing highlights are dotted around other parts of town. The area of Karama is famous for its markets and restaurants serving cheap south-Asian dinners; Satwa is home to some of the best people-watching in the city, and the dusty industrial park, Al Quoz, hosts several of the most cutting-edge art galleries in the region.

Gallery Isabelle Van Den Eynde
04 323 5052

Al Serkal Ave, Street 8, Al Quoz Industrial 1 ivde.net

This progressive art gallery represents Middle Eastern artists and is partnered with galleries in Europe. The result is a hub where collectors can source artwork and get advice on everything from finance to framing. Even if you're not in the market to buy, there are exhibitions by a steadily growing roster of talent. Open 10:00 to 19:00 Saturday to Thursday. **Map** 1 E3 **Metro** Noor Islamic Bank

Global Village
04 362 4114

Nr Arabian Ranches, Emirates
Rd, Dubailand globalvillage.ae

Between the end of October and March a huge plot of paved desert outside of Dubai blossoms into a celebration of multiculturalism and fairground fun. There are plenty of big rides and action-orientated shows to entertain the family, but the main attraction is the shopping. Vendors come from over 45 countries in Africa, Asia and the Middle East to showcase their cultural wares. Much of the clothing, furniture and decorations on sale are less-than-attractive, but each area has shops full of knick-knacks you can't find anywhere else.

Map 1 E6 **Metro** Mall Of The Emirates

Iranian Mosque

Al Wasl Road, Jumeira 1

Non-Muslims can't enter the Iranian Mosque, but it's still worth admiring (and photographing) from the outside. The blue mosaic tiling, pillars, arches and elaborate minarets are typical of Persian architecture, making this one of the most photogenic sights in Dubai. The mosque also serves as a stunning counterpoint to some of the modern places of worship you'll see elsewhere in the city.

Map 1 H2 **Metro** World Trade Centre

The Jam Jar   04 341 7303

Nr Dubai Garden Center,
   Street 17A, Al Quoz Industrial 3   thejamjardubai.com

The Jam Jar is injecting a little culture to Sheikh Zayed Road. This small, bright gallery offers wannabe Picassos the chance to let their creative juices flow. Everything from paints to brushes is provided and prices start from Dhs.195. Open 10:00 to 20:00 Monday to Thursday and Saturday, 14:00 to 20:00 on Friday and closed Sunday. **Map** 1 E3 **Metro** First Gulf Bank

Karama

Primarily a residential area consisting of relatively low-cost flats in low-rise apartment blocks, Karama is well known for having something for everyone. It has a great shopping area, which is particularly notorious for its imitation goods, and the popular Karama Complex (p.195). Karama's merchants are a far cry from their mall counterparts and offer a challenge if you like practising your haggling skills. There's a great range of inexpensive restaurants serving tasty Indian and Pakistani cuisine, including Saravana Bhavan (p.288) and Karachi Darbar (04 334 7272).

Map 5 A4 **Metro** Al Karama

Opera Gallery

04 323 0909

Dubai International Financial
 Centre (DIFC), Trade Centre

operagallery.com

Part of an international chain, Opera Gallery opened in 2008 in Dubai International Financial Centre. It has a permanent collection of art on display and for sale, mainly European and Chinese, with visiting exhibitions changing throughout the year. The permanent collection also includes several masterpieces, so look out for the odd Dali or Picasso.

Map 2 D2 **Metro** Financial Centre

Plant Street

Nr Satwa Rd & Al Wasl Rd, Al Satwa

Famous for pots and plants, pet shops, fabric shops and hardware outlets, Plant Street is another spot that hasn't changed much since the beginning of Dubai's boom. Head

Global Village

here on a Saturday evening to soak up the atmosphere, but women are advised to cover up to avoid being stared at.
Map 1 H2 **Metro** Trade Centre

The Third Line

04 341 1367

Nr Times Square, Al Quoz Industrial 1   thethirdline.com

One of the leading lights of the Dubai art scene, The Third Line gallery in Al Quoz hosts exhibitions by artists originating from or working in the Middle East. There are indoor and outdoor spaces for shows, many of which have caught the eye of both local and international collectors. The gallery is open Saturday to Thursday 10:00 to 19: 00; it is closed on Fridays. **Map** 1 F3 **Metro** Noor Islamic Bank

Further Out

The United Arab Emirates offers visitors some spectacular sights, from modern cities to ancient forts, and mountain pools to seemingly infinite deserts.

If you are on holiday in Dubai for longer than a few days, you should definitely build time into your schedule to explore the rest of the country. Hire a car or book a tour and hit the road: this part of the world has a lot to offer, and many of the sights are just a short drive away. Close to Dubai, nature lovers should check out Ras Al Khor Wildlife Sanctuary (Ras Al Khor Road, 04 606 6822), the only nature reserve within the city and a great place for bird watchers, with 1,500 flamingos. Once outside the urban sprawl you'll quickly be surrounded by rolling sand dunes, wandering camels and imposing mountains. Quite simply, heading out of Dubai to the other cities and emirates can be hugely rewarding and will add a worthy cultural perspective to your time in the UAE.

Abu Dhabi

Dubai is sometimes mistaken as the capital of the UAE, but that honour actually belongs to Abu Dhabi. Oil was discovered there before Dubai (1958 compared with 1966) and today it accounts for 10% of the world's known crude oil reserves, making it one of the richest cities on earth. It is home to a growing number of renowned hotels, a selection of shiny shopping malls and a sprinkling of culture in the form

THE UAE'S FIRST
MEGA WATERPARK

43 rides, slides and attractions.

Prepare for thrills, spills and laughter. Raise your heartbeat on the world's biggest tornado, board the planet's longest water coaster with laser effects, and shake up your senses on the world's first rattling waterslide. From adrenaline rushes, laidback lazy rivers, or shopping in the souk, there's something for the whole family. **Live the ultimate water adventure. Visit yaswaterworld.com**

YAS ISLAND

of heritage sites and souks. Travellers to the city shouldn't miss the 22,000sqm Sheikh Zayed Grand Mosque (szgmc.ae). Emirates Palace (emiratespalace.com) is another must-do: the stunning hotel houses several excellent restaurants and is well worth the visit for the architecture alone. Off the coast, Yas Island is a thrill-seeker's delight: in addition to the annual Formula 1 race, other events and driving experiences take place year-round at Yas Marina Circuit, while Ferrari World (ferrariworldabudhabi.com), a theme park, features petrol-fumed attractions of every kind and Yas Waterworld (yaswaterworld.com), a brand-new waterpark, aquatic thrills of all manner. Nearby is Saadiyat Island, a holiday paradise with a handful of classy hotels and resorts that include the luxurious Monte-Carlo Beach Club (montecarlobeachclub.ae). South-west of Abu Dhabi is the Liwa oasis, where the spectacular dunes are a photographer's dream. Liwa lies at the edge of the Rub Al Khali (Empty Quarter), one of the largest sand deserts in the world.

Al Ain

Al Ain is a city of great historic significance in the UAE thanks to its strategic location on ancient trading routes between Oman and the Gulf, and because of its fertile oases. The birthplace of the late, revered Sheikh Zayed, Al Ain is known as the Garden City, and is filled with several date plantations and pockets of greenery. These oases are lovely places to explore; drive around the networks of walled, cobbled roads, park up, and wander through the lush green plantations, complete with working falaj irrigation systems. You might

even get to taste some fresh fruit if you stumble across some harvested bounty (be sure to ask permission from the picker before you pop one in your mouth though). Next to the main Al Ain Oasis is the interesting Al Ain Palace Museum (03 751 7755, adach.ae), which illustrates various aspects of life in the UAE. Al Ain Zoo (03 782 8188, awpr.ae) is a nature-lover's dream and easily one of the city's best attractions. Conservation is the keyword here, with natural habitats recreated to be as near to the real thing as possible, and you can get the whole family up close to animals including giraffes, zebras and rhinos. For a great view over the city and expansive desert landscape, take a scenic drive up Jebel Hafeet. The winding road rises right to the summit, where you'll find the Mercure Grand Jebel Hafeet hotel – a great place for a refreshing drink with a terrific view (03 783 8888, mercure.com). At the foothill of the mountain you'll find Wadi Adventure (wadiadventure.ae), which offers a range of adrenaline-pumping activities such as whitewater rafting and kayaking.

East Coast

Even if you're only in the UAE for a short time, a trip to the East Coast is a must. You can get there in less than two hours.

The diving is considered better than that off Dubai's coast, mainly because of increased visibility. Snoopy Island off Dibba's coast is a favourite spot for snorkelling. The East Coast is home to a few interesting spots, many of which are free to explore. The site of the oldest mosque in the UAE, Bidiyah, is roughly half way down the East Coast, north of

Khor Fakkan. The building is believed to date back to the middle of the 15th century and was restored in 2003. The village is considered one of the oldest settlements on the East Coast, which is thought to have been inhabited since 3000BC. Located at the northernmost point of the East Coast, Dibba is made up of three fishing villages, each coming under a different jurisdiction: Sharjah, Fujairah, and Oman. The villages share an attractive bay and excellent diving locations. The Hajar Mountains provide a wonderful backdrop to the public beaches. Further north across the border into Oman is Khasab, a great base for exploring the inlets and unspoilt waters of Musandam. You can stay at the Golden Tulip Khasab Hotel Resort (+968 2 673 0777; goldentulipkhasab.com), which can organise dhow cruises and dolphin watching, or at the luxurious Six Senses Zighy Bay (+968 2 673 5555; sixsenses.com). Further south on the coast lies Fujairah, the youngest of the seven emirates. Overlooking the atmospheric old town is a fort that is reportedly about 300 years old. The surrounding hillsides are dotted with more such ancient forts and watchtowers, which add an air of mystery and charm. Dubai residents often use Fujairah as a base for exploring the rest of the coast. Hotels include Le Meridien Al Aqah Beach Resort (09 244 9000; lemeridien-alaqah.com), and Radisson Blu Resort, Fujairah (09 244 9700; radissonblu.com). Khor Kalba sits just south of Fujairah. It's the most northerly mangrove forest in the world, and home to a variety of plant, marine and birdlife not found anywhere else in the UAE. A canoe tour by Desert Rangers (p.145) is the best way to reach the heart of the reserve.

Hatta

The road leading to Hatta from Dubai (E44) is a trip in itself. Watch as the sand gradually changes from beige to dark orange and then disappears, only to be replaced by jagged mountains. The famous Big Red sand dune lies on this road, and is a popular spot for dune driving in 4WDs or quad bikes.

Hatta is a small town, nestled at the foot of the Hajar Mountains, about 100km from Dubai city and 10km from the Dubai-Oman border. It is home to the oldest fort in Dubai emirate, which was built in 1790. You'll also see several watchtowers on the surrounding hills. On the drive you'll pass a row of carpet shops, ideal for putting your bargaining skills into practice. The town itself has a sleepy, relaxed feel, and includes the Heritage Village (04 852 1374), which charts the area's 3,000 year history and includes a 200 year-old mosque and the fortress built by Sheikh Maktoum bin Hasher Al Maktoum in 1896, which is now used as a weaponry museum.

The Hatta Fort Hotel's (04 809 9333, jaresortshotels.com) bungalow-style rooms feature stunning Arabic decor and the resort has plenty of sports and leisure facilities, including shooting and mini-golf.

Beyond the village and into the mountains are the Hatta Pools, where you can see deep, strangely shaped canyons carved out by rushing floodwater. For tours see p.144.

The trail towards the pools is graded, so a two-wheel drive car and some skilled driving should be enough to get you there. To get to the pools from the Dubai-Hatta road, take a right at the fort roundabout, then left towards the Heritage Village, another left at the roundabout, and then the first

Nothing stops you here!

DREAMLAND AQUA PARK

Itihad Road E11, Umm Al Quwain,
Through Emirates Road E311, Exit 103, Tel: 06 7681888

Fridays and Public Holidays are reserved for families,
pre-booked groups or special pass holders

For the latest updates �f 🖸 Dreamland Aqua Park

Take a break. There is something for everyone at
Dreamland Aqua Park. Indulge in absolute fun at the
amazing 250,000 sq.m. fun land. Over 30 thrilling
rides, crazy slides, unlimited wet & dry attractions,
along with ample sporting and overnight camping
activities. Adding to the thrill is the Mini Zoo; not to
mention, great meeting and team building facilities.
So, splash. Play. Get recharged!

For SPECIAL OFFERS visit
www.dreamlanduae.com

main right. After driving through a second village, the tarmac will end and you will see a gravel track on your right.

Northern Emirates

North of Dubai and Sharjah are Ajman, Umm Al Quwain and Ras Al Khaimah. These three emirates are much smaller in size than Dubai and Abu Dhabi and are also less developed.

Ajman is the smallest of the emirates, but its proximity to Dubai and Sharjah has enabled it to grow considerably. It was once known as one of the largest dhow building centres in the region, and while it is mainly modern boats that emerge from the yards these days, you can still catch a glimpse of a traditionally built dhow sailing out to sea. Ajman also has some great beaches and a pleasant corniche. Much of the nightlife revolves around the Ajman Kempinski Hotel & Resort (06 714 5555, kempinski.com).

Umm Al Quwain has the smallest population and little has changed over the years, though it is home to the expansive Dreamland Aqua Park (dreamlanduae.com). Two of the most interesting activities Umm Al Quwain has to offer are crab hunting and mangrove tours. The Flamingo Beach Resort (06 765 0000, flamingoresort.ae) offers both tours.

Ras Al Khaimah is the most northerly of the seven emirates but you can make the trip from Dubai in around an hour on the Emirates Road. With the jagged Hajar Mountains rising just behind the city, and the Arabian Gulf stretching out from the shore, RAK has some of the best scenery in the UAE. A creek divides the city into the old town and the newer Al Nakheel district. For a day trip, you should go to the souk in the old town and the National Museum of Ras Al Khaimah (07 233 3411, rasalkhaimahtourism.com). This is a good starting point for exploring the surrounding countryside and visiting the ancient sites of Ghalilah and Shimal.

Sharjah

Before Dubai's rise to prominence as a trading and tourism hotspot, neighbouring Sharjah was one of the wealthiest towns in the region, with settlers earning their livelihood from fishing, pearling and trade. Sharjah's commitment to art, culture and preserving its traditional heritage is well known throughout the Arab world and the city is home to several museums that are well worth a visit; see sharjahmuseums. ae for full details of these. Sharjah is built around Khalid Lagoon (popularly known as the creek), and the surrounding Buhairah Corniche is a popular spot for an evening stroll. From various points on the lagoon, small dhows can be hired to see the lights of the city from the water. The Heritage Area (06 569 3999, sharjahtourism.ae) is a fascinating old walled city, home to numerous museums and the traditional Souk Al Arsah. The nearby Arts Area is a treat for art lovers with galleries and more museums. A must is Al Qasba (06 556 0777, alqasba.ae), which has performance spaces and waterside restaurants. Another worthy stop-off is the Sharjah Natural History & Botanical Museum (06 531 1411, sharjahmuseums.ae). Shoppers shouldn't miss the beautiful Central Souk, also known as the Blue Souk. The two buildings contain more than 600 shops selling gold and knick-knacks. This is one of the best places in the UAE to buy carpets.

Oman

Just a few hours from Dubai, you'll find the countless attractions of Oman. It's a peaceful and breathtaking country, with history, culture and spectacular scenery. The capital, Muscat, has enough attractions to keep you busy for a short break, including beautiful beaches, some great restaurants and cafes, and the mesmerising old souk at Mutrah. Out of the capital, you will find many historic old towns and forts, and some of the most stunning mountain and wadi scenery in the region. Salalah in the south has the added bonus of being cool and wet in the summer. Isolated from the rest of the country, on the tip of the Arabian Peninsula, is the Omani enclave of Musandam. With its jagged mountains and fjord-like inlets, it has the moniker 'the Norway of the Middle East' and is a must-visit if you are in Dubai for any serious length of time.

Ras Al Jinz is a small fishing village on the Ras Al Hadd Turtle Reserve. The protected beach is where endangered green turtles come to nest and visitors can see the huge turtles by booking a guided tour with Ras Al Jinz Scientific & Visitor Center (+968 9 655 0606/0707, rasaljinz-turtlereserve. com) which has a small guesthouse, restaurant and gift shop.

A flight from Dubai to Muscat takes 45 minutes, but when you factor in check-in times and customs it's not much quicker than driving. There are daily flights from Dubai with Emirates and Oman Air, while Air Arabia flies from Sharjah. Regular flights to Salalah from Dubai are also available. It is possible to drive to Musandam from Dubai in around three hours, but make sure your hire car insurance covers Oman. For further information see the *Oman Mini Visitors' Guide*.

TOUR Dubai

DHOW CRUISE
Guided Tours

DUBAI MARINA

One hour cruise with Commentary every hour from 10.30 - 5.30pm

Also Dinner Cruises & Fishing Charters
04 3368406/07/09 admin@tour-dubai.com

Tours & Sightseeing

Whether it be by plane, boat or 4WD, taking a tour is a fun and efficient way to see a different side of the Emirates.

Navigating the city by taxi or Metro can be pretty easy, but exploring the surrounding areas often proves a bit more difficult without the help of a guide. Boat tours are a great way to see the city from afar while enjoying the clear Gulf waters; helicopter and plane tours give the most extensive look at the growing city; and bus tours offer plenty of information and more user-friendly schedules.

No visitor should leave without experiencing a desert safari of some sort. Expert drivers blast 4WDs up, down and around massive dunes while passing old Bedouin villages and pointing out incredible natural attractions. Mountain safaris lead passengers through the narrow wadis of the Hajar Mountains. Most driving safaris include pickup from your hotel and lunch. Some end the day of driving at a replica Bedouin camp where passengers can watch a belly dancer, eat Arabic delicacies and smoke shisha. Some operators run overnight safaris that combine half-day treks with a driving adventure.

While most of the companies listed below offer a wide range of experiences, some are more specialised. Both Aerogulf Services and Seawings concentrate on plane tours, Balloon Adventures is the city's main balloon ride operator, Big Bus Tours is the premier bus tour provider, and Bristol Middle East concentrates on boat and yacht tours.

Tour Operators

Absolute Adventure	04 345 9900	adventure.ae
Aerogulf Services Company	04 220 0331	aerogulfservices.com
Alpha Tours	04 294 9888	alphatoursdubai.com
Arabian Adventures	04 303 4888	arabian-adventures.com
Balloon Adventures Emirates	04 285 4949	ballooning.ae
Big Bus Tours	04 340 7709	bigbustours.com
Bristol Middle East Yacht Solution	04 366 3538	bristol-middleeast.com
Desert Adventures Tourism	04 450 2224	desertadventures.com
Desert Rangers	04 357 2200	desertrangers.com
Dubai Tourist & Travel Services	04 336 7727	dubai-travel.ae
Gulf Ventures	04 404 5880	gulfventures.ae
Knight Tours	04 343 7725	knighttours.ae
Net Tours	04 602 8888	nettours-uae.com
Oasis Palm Tourism	04 262 8889	opdubai.com
Omeir Travel Agency	04 337 7727	omeir.com
Orient Tours	04 282 8238	orienttours.ae
Seawings	**04** 807 0708	seawings.ae
Sunflower Tours	04 334 5554	sunflowerdubai.com
Tour Dubai	04 336 8407	tour-dubai.com
Travco	04 336 6643	travcotravel.ae
Wonder Bus Tours	04 359 5656	wonderbustours.net

Sports & Spas

Active Dubai

Dubai has a wealth of spas, sports and resorts dedicated to the art of relaxation.

It is not just shops and beaches that attract visitors to Dubai. Numerous world-class sporting events take place in the city throughout the year, drawing crowds of residents and tourists alike. The Dubai World Cup is the richest horse race in the world, the Dubai Rugby Sevens regularly pulls in crowds in excess of 70,000 and the Dubai Duty Free Tennis Championships see the world's leading players compete in an intimate setting.

Dubai is also home to several excellent golf courses, many designed by leading figures such as Robert Trent Jones II, Colin Montgomerie and Nick Faldo.

Traditional Arabian sports, such as camel racing and falconry, offer an interesting perspective on local heritage, and should not be missed.

A combination of Arabian Gulf shoreline and the vast expanses of desert just outside the city make Dubai a great adventure sports destination: from kitesurfing and diving to dune driving and sand skiing, there are many opportunities for unique and exciting sports activities.

All this activity aside, those who are seeking blissful holidays spent relaxing and rejuvenating will find a collection of world-class spas offering a range of unique treatments in luxurious surroundings, usually at surprisingly reasonable prices.

Clockwise from top left: climbing Fossil Rock, underwater life, Dubai Tennis Championships

Sports & Activities

Miles of sand dunes, clear seas, classic Arabian heritage and superb sports facilities: holidays in Dubai are packed with unique sporting opportunities.

Dhow Charters

Al Boom Tourist Village

04 324 3000

Nr Al Garhoud Bridge, Umm Hurair   alboom.ae

Al Boom Tourist Village operates nine dhow boats on the creek, ranging from single-deckers with room for 20 people, right up to the huge triple-decker Mumtaz, which can take 300 passengers. It offers a variety of packages, with prices varying accordingly. As well as the usual dinner cruises, late-night trips can also be arranged.
Map 4 C6 **Metro** Healthcare City

Khasab Travel & Tours

04 266 9950

Warba Centre, Al Muraqqabat   khasabtours.com

This operator organises day cruises in Khasab, Oman (including car transfers from Dubai). The route follows the rugged Musandam coastline, which has been dubbed the 'Norway of Arabia,' offering fantastic photo opportunities: you'll pass small fishing villages in incredibly remote locations and will (hopefully) also see dolphins and turtles. Prices start at Dhs.200 per adult for a full day, including lunch and refreshments. **Map** 4 E4 **Metro** Abu Baker Al Siddique

Golf

With an ideal climate for most of the year, golf is a popular sport in Dubai and the number of international-standard courses has increased rapidly. Although plans for a Tiger Woods designed course were cancelled, recent additions to Dubai's golf scene include courses designed by such names as South Africa's 'Big Easy' Ernie Els. Dubai Golf operates a central reservation system at dubaigolf.com.

Al Badia Golf Club By Intercontinental Dubai Festival City

04 601 0101
albadiagolfclub.ae

Dubai Festival City

World-renowned golf course designer Robert Trent Jones II is behind the InterContinental's offering. Lying at the heart of Dubai Festival City, beside the creek, the resort enjoys great views across the city. The 7,303 yard par 72 Championship Course has a plush clubhouse and extensive water features.

Map 1 J4 **Metro** Emirates

Arabian Ranches Golf Club

04 366 3000

Emirates Rd,
Arabian Ranches
arabianranchesgolfdubai.com

Designed by Ian Baker-Finch in association with Nicklaus Design, this par 72 grass course uses the natural desert terrain and features indigenous shrubs and bushes. You must have an official handicap to play, but can reserve a tee-off time six days in advance. Facilities include a golf academy with floodlit driving range, an extensive short game practice area, and GPS on all golf carts. **Map** 1 D5

Dubai Creek Golf & Yacht Club

04 295 6000

Nr Deira City Centre, Baniyas Rd,
  Port Saeed

dubaigolf.com

The par 71 course was designed by Thomas Björn and is open
to all players with a valid handicap certificate. Those who are
new to the game are encouraged to train with PGA qualified
instructors at the academy. There is also a nine-hole par three
course, a floodlit range and extensive short game practice
areas. The iconic clubhouse features several dining favourites
and two pro shops. **Map** 4 C6 **Metro** Deira City Centre

The Els Club Dubai

04 425 1010

Emirates Rd, Dubai Sports City

elsclubdubai.com

Designed by Ernie Els, this 18 hole course that stretches
7,538 yards is very popular among Dubai's golfers. A massive
Mediterranean clubhouse is still under construction, but a
temporary clubhouse serves members and visitors in the
meantime. **Map** 1 C4 **Metro** Dubai Internet City

Emirates Golf Club

04 380 2222

Off Sheikh Zayed Rd, Emirates Living

dubaigolf.com

At Emirates Golf Club you can choose from two 18 hole
courses: the 7,301 yard, par 72 Majlis Course – the first grass
course in the Middle East and venue for the Dubai Desert
Classic – or the Faldo Course designed by Nick Faldo and IMG
Design. The club has a Peter Cowen Golf Academy, along with
two driving ranges, practice areas and clubhouse.
Map 3 B2 **Metro** Nakheel

Jebel Ali Golf Resort
04 814 5555
Nr Palm Jebel Ali, Waterfront
jaresortshotels.com

Situated in the landscaped gardens of the Jebel Ali Golf Resort & Spa, this nine-hole, par 36 course offers views of the Arabian Gulf. Renowned for its good condition all year, the course is also home to the Jebel Ali Golf Resort & Spa Challenge, the opener for the Omega Dubai Desert Classic (p.163).

Montgomerie Golf Club
04 390 5600
The Address Montgomerie Dubai,
Emirates Living
themontgomerie.com

Designed by Colin Montgomerie and Desmond Muirhead, the 18 hole, par 72 course has some unique characteristics, including the 656 yard 18th hole. The facilities include a driving range and a swing analysis studio.

Map 3 B3 Metro Nakheel

Hot Air Ballooning & Parasailing

Balloon Adventures Emirates (04 285 4949), Amigos Balloons (04 289 9295, amigos-balloons.com) and Desert Rangers (04 357 2200) offer trips across the desert in a hot air balloon. Journeys with Amigos Balloons cost Dhs.950 per person and set off from a variety of locations – you can also go for a private flight for two for Dhs.5,500. If you'd like an aerial view of the Palm Jumeirah but can't afford a balloon, then try parasailing. The Sheraton Jumeirah Beach Resort (04 399 5533) has a watersports and an activity centre, and Nautica 1992 (050 426 2415) operates from the Habtoor Grand. Summertime Marine Sports (04 257 3084) also offers flights from the open beach near Le Meridien Mina Seyahi hotel (04 399 3333). All use specially designed boats with winches and a launch pad on the back, so you don't have to sprint down the beach to get airborne. You can expect to pay around Dhs.250 for a 15 to 20 minute ride or Dhs.350 for the tandem option – however, prices vary depending on the length and option of the ride.

Motorsports

The UAE deserts provide ideal locations for rallying, and many events are organised throughout the year by the Emirates Motor Sports Federation (emsf.ae). The high-profile Abu Dhabi Desert Challenge (uaedesertchallenge.com) is one of the top events in World Cup Cross Country Rallying. Other events throughout the year include the Spring Desert Rally (4WD), Peace Rally (saloons), Jeep Jamboree (safari), Drakkar Noir 1000 Dunes Rally (4WD), Shell Festival Parade, Audi Driving Skills (driving challenge) and Federation Rally (4WD). Yas Island (yasisland.ae), located a short drive away in Abu Dhabi, is home to various attractions and amenities to delight any petrolhead. In addition to the annual Formula 1 Etihad Airways Grand Prix, the Yas Marina Circuit (yasmarinacircuit.com) hosts several other motorsports events throughout the year. Also on Yas Island, the Ferrari World (ferrariworldabudhabi.com) theme park features high-octane attractions of all manner.

Dubai Autodrome
Emirates Rd, MotorCity

04 367 8700
dubaiautodrome.com

The Dubai Autodrome (part of Dubailand, on Emirates Road) is the home of motorsport in Dubai. It has six different track

configurations, including a 5.39km FIA-sanctioned GP circuit, premium pit facilities and a 7,000 seat grandstand. The venue hosts events throughout the year, including rounds of the FIA GT Championships. You can experience the thrill of driving on a racetrack with the guidance of qualified instructors. A range of packages and experiences is offered, including a track taster session in Audi TTs with prices starting from Dhs.825. Wannabe Vettels of any age can burn rubber at the kartdrome. After a safety briefing, you'll take to your powerful 390cc kart (there are smaller 120cc karts for the kids) and hit the tarmac on the exciting 1.2km circuit. Map 1 D5

Skiing & Snowboarding

When temperatures outside are melting your sunglasses, you can go sub-zero with a visit to Ski Dubai (800 386). The huge tube extending behind and above the Mall Of The Emirates (p.207) is home to five slopes to suit all skill levels, from gentle beginner slopes to the world's first indoor 'black' run. The attractions also include the unique opportunity to get up and close with some irresistibly cute resident penguins. The slope itself has both chair lifts and tow lifts, and there's a well-stocked retail shop selling skis, boards, and clothing. Strict rules ensure only suitably skilled skiers and boarders can take to the slopes, but beginners can get take part too by booking a lesson with one of the qualified instructors. Entrance to the Snow Park is Dhs.130 for adults and Dhs.120 for children. Prices for a two-hour Ski Slope Pass start at Dhs.180 for adults and Dhs.150 for kids; the prices include equipment and clothing (except gloves).

Wadi & Dune Bashing

Most car rental agencies offer visitors 4WDs capable of desert driving. If renting a 4WD, make sure you get the details of the insurance plan, as many rental insurers won't cover damage caused by off-roading. Dune bashing, or desert driving, is one of the toughest challenges for both car and driver, but once you have mastered it, it's a lot of fun.

If you do venture out into the desert, it is a good idea to have at least one experienced driver and one other car to help tow you out if you get stuck. Most major tour companies offer a range of desert and mountain safaris if you'd rather leave the driving to the professionals.

Driving in wadis is usually a bit more straightforward. Wadis are (usually) dry gullies, carved through the rock by rushing floodwaters, following the course of seasonal rivers. The main safety precaution to take when wadi bashing is to keep your eyes open for rare, but not impossible, thunder storms developing. The wadis can fill up quickly and you will need to make your way to higher ground pretty fast to avoid flash floods. For further information and tips on off-road driving in the UAE, check out the *UAE Off-Road Explorer*.

Watersports & Diving

Most beachside hotels offer both guests and visitors a range of watersports, including sea kayaking, sailing and windsurfing. Some hotels require that non-guests pay beach fees in order to access the facilities, while others will let you enter the beach area for free if you make a reservation at the watersports desk beforehand. Contact the Habtoor Grand

The Dubai sports scene is amazingly varied

Resort (04 399 5000) and Le Meridien Mina Seyahi (04 399 3333) for pricing and availability of various watersports – both hotels have comprehensive facilities located along the 1.7km stretch of beach in JBR (p.104) and whether it's parasailing, kayaking or taking a banana boat ride you're after, it's likely to be on offer here.

Simulated Fun

Dubai's malls have fantastic entertainment; try sky diving at Playnation, Mirdif City Centre (p.210) or for the biggest selection, head to SEGA Republic at The Dubai Mall (p.204) which has motor racing, a jungle safari and a bobsleigh simulator for big (and little) kids to try.

Diving is popular and the clear waters off the coast are home to a variety of marine species, coral life and even shipwrecks. You'll see some exotic fish and possibly moray eels, small sharks, barracuda, sea snakes and stingrays.

Most of the wrecks are located on the west coast of the UAE, while the flora and fauna can be seen on the east side, in Fujairah (p.136). Another option for diving enthusiasts is a trip to Musandam. Part of the Sultanate of Oman (p.142), it is often described as the 'Norway of the Middle East' due to its many inlets and cliffs that plunge directly into the sea. Sheer wall dives with strong currents and clear waters are more suitable for advanced divers, while the huge bays with their calm waters and bountiful shallow reefs are ideal for the less experienced. Courses are offered under the usual international training organisations. More details on specific dives and sites can be found in the *UAE Underwater Explorer*.

Al Boom Diving

04 342 2993

Nr Iranian Hospital, Al Wasl Rd, Jumeira 1   alboomdiving.com

Al Boom Diving is a purpose-built school with a fully outfitted diving shop. A variety of courses are held both here and at the company's PADI Gold Palm Resort at Le Meridien Al Aqah Beach Resort (09 244 9000) near Fujairah on the East Coast. For aquatic thrills right in the heart of the city, Al Boom Diving also offers the chance to dive with the sharks in The Dubai Mall's gigantic aquarium (p.99).

Map 1 H2 **Metro** Emirates Towers

The Pavilion Dive Centre

04 406 8827

Jumeirah Beach Hotel, Umm Suqeim 3   jumeirah.com

This centre is run by PADI course directors, who offer courses for beginners through to instructors. Daily dive charters for certified divers are available in Dubai, and trips to the Musandam peninsula in Oman can be organised upon request. Two dives with full equipment are priced at Dhs.450 in Dubai or Dhs.700 in Musandam (including transport and lunch). **Map** 3 E1 **Metro** Mall Of The Emirates

Wadi Adventure

03 781 8422

Off Al Ain Fayda Rd, Al Ain   wadiadventure.ae

Located on the foothills of Al Ain's (p.134) Jebel Hafeet mountain, this new resort is worth the 90 minute car ride from Dubai if you're a fan of adrenaline-pumping watersports. In addition to three world-class white water rafting and kayaking runs, there's also a huge surf pool. Entry costs Dhs.100, activities are charged separately.

Spectator Sports

Dubai has the best line-up of international sport in the region, with world-class tennis, golf and horse racing among the highlights.

A good range of sporting events is organised in Dubai and the emirate is steadily backing more big international events that not only capture the local imagination, but also draw sporting enthusiasts from around the world. A big advantage is that crowds are smaller and tickets for larger events are more freely available than they would be in other countries, though you'll have to be quick. Horse racing, desert rallies and motorsports are very popular as are local sports like camel racing.

Camel Racing

This is a chance to see a truly traditional local sport. Races take place in the winter months and additional games are often held on public holidays. Races were previously held at the track

Camel Rides

Take a short camel ride along the beach near the Hilton Dubai Jumeirah or as part of a desert safari – it's a great way to experience this traditional mode of transport. The lumbering clumsiness of the camel standing up when you first hop on forms a marked contrast to the surprising smoothness of the ride itself.

at Nad Al Sheba, but this has closed to make way for Meydan City. To find the new location, head up the Al Ain Road, past the Dubai Outlet Mall, until you reach the Al Lisali exit. Turn right off this exit and you will see the track on your right. Races are usually held early on a Friday morning, but you should see camels being exercised during the day in the cooler months.

Golf

DP World Tour Championship

Jumeirah Golf Estates   dpworldtourchampionship.com

The Dubai World Championship is the grand finale of The Race to Dubai, the European Tour's season-long competition which features 50 tournaments in 27 destinations. This annual tournament runs for four days and is open to the leading 60 players in The Race to Dubai rankings after the 49th event, ensuring that the cream of the golf world qualifies for the chance to compete for a prize fund of $2.5 million. **Map** 1 B4

Omega Dubai Desert Classic   04 380 2112

Emirates Golf Club, Emirates Living   dubaidesertclassic.com

One of the highlights of the Dubai sporting calendar, this European PGA Tour competition is a popular winter event among both players and spectators. The tournament takes place at the end of January and start of February; see the website for more details. Top golfers who have previously competed in the event include Tiger Woods, Ernie Els and Henrik Stenson. **Map** 3 B2 **Metro** Nakheel

Horse Racing

Dubai Racing Club
Meydan Racecourse, Nad Al Sheba

04 327 0077
dubairacingclub.com

A visit to Dubai during the winter months is not complete without experiencing race night. For the past few years, the races have taken place at the impressively large, state-of-the-art racecourse in Meydan City. Featuring a 60,000 seat grandstand, a five-star hotel and several restaurants, it's as much a racecourse as an entertainment destination in its own right. Every March, the world's richest horse race, the Dubai World Cup, takes place here. You can see a slightly more raw form of horse racing at Jebel Ali racecourse (04 347 4914), near The Greens. **Map** 1 G4

Motorsports

Since 2009, Abu Dhabi has been hosting an annual Formula 1 World Championship, held at the new Yas Island Marina Circuit in Abu Dhabi. It's a high-profile three-day event; in addition to fast cars and high-octane thrills, the weekend usually includes concert performances by a number of big name entertainers to top off the experience. The event takes place in November; check formula1.com for the dates. The Dubai Autodrome (dubaiautodrome.com) is an FIA-approved circuit that hosts legs of international racing series. The Abu Dhabi Desert Challenge (abudhabidesertchallenge.com), which was previously known as the UAE Desert Challenge, is another popular event where motorbikes and 4WDs battle it out over the dunes.

Rugby

Emirates Airline Dubai Rugby Sevens   04 321 0008
The Sevens   dubairugby7s.com

One of the biggest events in the UAE, the Dubai Rugby
Sevens (dubairugby7s.com) attracts a huge crowd each year.
The two-day event is the first stop in the IRB Sevens World
Series and plays host to the top 16 Sevens teams in the world.
The first day of the event sees regional teams go head to
head, with the international teams joining the fray for the last
two days. As well as the international matches, you can also
watch social, youth and women's games at the event. Tickets
can sell out weeks in advance so plan early.

Tennis

Dubai Duty Free Tennis
Championships
The Aviation Club, Al Garhoud
dubaidutyfreetennischampionships.com

The Dubai Tennis Championships takes place every February
at The Aviation Club in Garhoud; it offers a great opportunity
to catch some of the top players in the game at close
quarters. The event is firmly established on the international
tennis calendar, and features both men's and ladies'
tournaments. Tickets for the later stages sell out in advance
so keep an eye out for sale details – entrance to some of the
earlier rounds can be bought on the day.

Map 4 D6 **Metro** GGICO

Out Of Dubai

Dubai may offer everything from sun to snow but there are interesting events held just outside of the emirate should you want to venture further afield.

Abu Dhabi Desert Challenge
02 296 1122
Empty Quarter, Abu Dhabi   abudhabidesertchallenge.ae

The Abu Dhabi Desert Challenge is a hot and heavy competition held in the desert around Abu Dhabi. The event sees motorbikes, 4WDs and quad bikes traverse the dunes on a five-day rally. The Desert Challenge takes place in a few different locations, including Moreeb Hill. Check the website for details of the routes – spectators are very welcome.

Abu Dhabi HSBC Golf Championship
—
Abu Dhabi Golf Club,
Abu Dhabi   abudhabigolfchampionship.com

With some of the biggest names in golf in attendance, the annual Abu Dhabi Golf Championship is a popular event. The European PGA Tour curtain-raiser is held at the Abu Dhabi Golf Club (02 558 8990, adgolfclub.com) in January; in addition to golf, there's children's entertainment, competitions and an array of food and beverage outlets.

Al Ain Aerobatic Show
800 555
Al Ain Intl Airport, Al Ain   alainaerobaticshow.com

This popular annual event, held every winter at Al Ain Airport, attracts thousands of spectators. The event features some incredible stunt flying with model aircrafts, helicopters, wingwalkers, gliders, and military and civilian planes. There is a festival atmosphere, with tents and displays, and children are well catered for with a play area and bouncy castles. There are a few places to get food but it may be worth packing a picnic.

Formula 1 Etihad Airways Abu Dhabi Grand Prix

Yas Marina Circuit, Abu Dhabi   yasmarinacircuit.com

Since 2009, the annual Formula 1 Etihad Airways Abu Dhabi Grand Prix has been a major event on the UAE sporting calendar. Fans of the sport get to enjoy a close view of the action on the world-class FIA sanctioned, 5.6km Yas Marina Circuit, and concerts by big name performers top off the experience. The race takes place on Yas Island, approximately one hour's drive from Dubai, in November.

Mubadala World Tennis Championship 04 493 8888

Abu Dhabi International Tennis Complex,
  Zayed Sports City, Abu Dhabi   mubadalawtc.com

Abu Dhabi's first international tennis championship was held in January 2009 and top seeds Roger Federer and Rafael Nadal are among the names to battle it out here. The three-day event features family attractions for spectators, as well as a series of tennis-based activities and tournaments during the run-up to the event, including the Community Cup. Day one sees the elimination round; day two hosts the semis, and day three climaxes with the final and consolation match. The event takes place over New Year's celebrations.

Spas

Take some time out from the city's frenetic pace to enjoy a massage, facial or hammam – you won't have to go far to find one.

A comprehensive range of treatments is on offer in the city and you can find spas offering anything from Balinese massage, hammams and Moroccan baths, to ayurvedic treatments and hot-stone therapy in Dubai's five-star hotels.

The price of treatments varies between spas, and while basic treatments like manicures and pedicures can be cheaper in the smaller spas and salons, you will often pay a high price for more exotic treatments in the upmarket hotels. Lesser known options are just as good and often cheaper. Jumeira has several smaller spas, treatment centres and nail salons, such as Elche (p.173), that cater for those on a more modest budget.

Spas will often offer set packages that combine a few treatments to make your visit more cost-effective. Compare packages between spas to get the best deal – and ask about their facilities as you will often be allowed to use the sauna, pool or Jacuzzi before or after your treatment.

Some spas only serve women, but others offer couples treatments or have separate areas for men. Grooming lounges like 1847 (p.169), which cater exclusively to men, are also increasingly popular.

1847

04 399 8989

Grosvenor House, Dubai Marina   thegroomingcompany.com

Considered the first dedicated 'grooming lounge' for men in the Middle East, 1847 offers manicures, professional shaves and massages in a decidedly manly setting. Several of the treatments take place in private studies, with personal LCD TVs. There is another lounge in The Boulevard at Emirates Towers (04 330 1847) and The Walk, Jumeirah Beach Residence (04 437 0252). **Map** 3 B1 **Metro** Dubai Marina

Ahasees Spa & Club

04 317 2333

Grand Hyatt Dubai, Umm Hurair   dubai.grand.hyatt.com

Although this is a relatively large spa, its atmosphere and attention to detail are spot on. The relaxation area is lit by rows of candles and the wet area (which has a Jacuzzi, plunge pool, steam room and spacious showers) is peppered with rose petals. A broad range of treatments are available, from facials designed to help preserve youthfulness, to massages using essential oils. **Map** 4 B6 **Metro** Healthcare City

Akaru Spa

04 282 8578

The Aviation Club, Al Garhoud   akaruspa.com

The autumnal colours, natural decor, wooden fittings and glass features create a truly tranquil retreat at this Garhoud favourite. Exotic treatments range from various specialised facials and wraps to microdermabrasion. During the cooler months, Akaru offers treatments on the rooftop terrace. **Map** 4 D6 **Metro** GGICO

Amara Spa Dubai

04 602 1234

Park Hyatt Dubai, Port Saeed   dubai.park.hyatt.com

Nestled in stunning surroundings on the banks of the Dubai
Creek, Amara Spa is a luxurious treat. The treatment rooms
act as your personal spa and, after being treated to one of
the fantastic facials or massages, you'll get to enjoy your own
private outdoor shower and relaxation area.

Map 4 D5 **Metro** GGICO

Angsana Spa & Health Club Dubai Marina

04 368 4356

Marina Walk, Dubai Marina   angsanaspa.com

Angsana Spa is a haven of Thai-style relaxation in the heart
of Dubai Marina. This is not among the flashy, five-star hotel
spas that have come to define the Dubai spa scene in some
parts of town; instead, you'll find a tranquil space with
impeccable attention to detail and skilled therapists to deliver
a soothing massage or beauty treat. Choose from a wide
range of treatments – the massages in particular are highly
recommended. **Map** 3 B1 **Metro** Dubai Marina

Assawan Spa & Health Club

04 301 7338

Burj Al Arab, Umm Suqeim   jumeirah.com

Located in the ultra-exclusive Burj Al Arab, this is as elaborate
a spot as you might expect. The spa has female-only and
mixed environments, including a gym with studios, saunas,
steam rooms, plunge pools and two infinity pools looking out
over the Arabian Gulf.

Map 3 E1 **Metro** Mall Of The Emirates

sensing the moment

Step into the tranquil sanctuary of Angsana Spa and let our spa therapists indulge you with our award-winning Asian therapies, designed to pamper the body and soothe the soul as you sense the moment.

Present this page at Angsana Spas Dubai to enjoy AED 100 off for any body massage. For Dubai Visitor Guide Readers Only. Valid till 31 December 2013.

Angsana Spa Arabian Ranches, Dubai
Tel: +971 4 361 8251
Email: spa-arabianranches@angsana.com

Angsana Spa Emirates Hills, Dubai
Tel: + 971 4 368 3222
Email: spa-emirateshills@angsana.com

Angsana Spa & Health Club Dubai Marina
Tel: + 971 4 368 4356
Email: spa-dubaimarina@angsana.com

Angsana Spa The Montgomerie, Dubai
Tel: +971 4 360 9322
Email: spa-montgomerie@angsana.com

ANGSANA
Spa

angsanaspa.com

B/Attitude
04 399 8888

Grosvenor House,
Dubai Marina
grosvenorhouse-dubai.com

Sister venue to Buddha Bar (p308), this stylish spa oozes
Oriental chic. Dark colours and soothing DJ tunes set the
scene and the treatments range from Eastern massages
to Ayurvedic therapies; Swiss Bellefontaine facials are also
available. **Map** 3 B1 **Metro** Dubai Marina

Cleopatra's Spa & Wellness
04 324 7700

Wafi, Umm Hurair
wafi.com

Cleopatra's Spa may not have the grand entrance that some
hotel spas share, but what it lacks in ostentation it makes up
for in other ways. The relaxation area is an ancient Egyptian
affair with drapes, silk cushions and majlis-style seats. The spa
menu features massages and facials, body wraps and anti-
ageing treatments. **Map** 4 B5 **Metro** Healthcare City

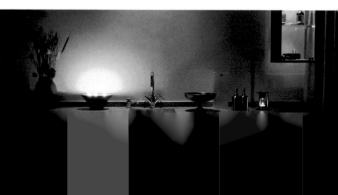

Elche Natural Beauty Retreat

04 349 4942

Villa 42, Nr Jumeirah Plaza, St 10C, Jumeira 1   elche.ae

Elche utilises the healing potential of herbs, fruit and flowers in its modern scientific methods. Set in a walled garden, this elegant retreat is warm and peaceful, with the entire experience tailored to the individual. You will also receive a client evaluation at the end of your treatment and can even have your makeup done by a professional.

Map 1 G2 **Metro** Al Jafiliya

Heavenly Spa By Westin Dubai Mina Seyahi

The Westin Dubai Mina Seyahi Beach   04 511 7901
 Resort & Marina, Al Sufouh 1   westinminaseyahi.com

Similar to other luxury spas in the immediate area, the service here leaves nothing to be desired. The contemporary decor still manages to feel warm and inviting, helping to clear your mind for the gorgeous treatments that await, which includes a fabulous four-handed Heavenly Massage.

Map 3 B1 **Metro** Nakheel

Man/Age

04 435 5780

The Walk, Jumeirah Beach Residence,
 Dubai Marina   managespa.com

This luxury men's spa offers all male grooming essentials – the spa menu includes everything from haircuts and shaving to manicures, massages and facials. There's also a Moroccan bath for a relaxing treat with local flair. A second branch is located in Media City (04 437 0868).

Map 3 A1 **Metro** Dubai Marina

Akaru Spa

Mandara Spa
04 501 8888

The H Hotel Dubai, Trade Centre 1
mandaraspa.com

Although this is one of the newer additions to Dubai's luxury spa scene, Mandara Spa has an established feel. The epicentre of the elegantly decorate luxury spa is a circular, cocoon-like chamber which contains a grand Jacuzzi pool, and from here you'll find your way to the communal changing room, sauna, steam room and atmospheric treatment rooms. Many of the body therapies on offer start with a foot washing ritual, and the quality of service is evident – nowhere more so than in the four-hands massage which is executed with expert synchronicity. An excellent option within easy reach from the financial district. **Map** 2 E1 **Metro** World Trade Centre

One&Only Private Spa
04 440 1040

One&Only The Palm,
Palm Jumeirah
oneandonlyresorts.com

The emphasis in this serene setting is on understated decor, with plenty of neutral colours and natural light. The relaxation room is a haven of tranquillity and an ideal spot to savour the sensations after your treatment. Its speciality is the 'canyon love stone therapy', an energy-balancing massage using warm and cool stones. **Map** 3 B1 **Metro** Nakheel

Oriental Hammam
04 315 2130

One&Only Royal Mirage,
Al Sufouh 1
oneandonlyresorts.com

This is the ultimate in Arabian luxury. The surroundings are elegant but not overly opulent, with a warm traditional feel.

Mandara Spa

The hammam and spa is an impressive area with mosaic-covered arches and intricate carvings on the high domes. The 50 minute treatment involves being bathed, steamed, and washed with traditional black soap. It may sound invasive, but it is a wonderfully invigorating treatment.

Map 3 B1 **Metro** Nakheel

The Ritz-Carlton Spa Dubai

The Ritz-Carlton, Dubai Marina

04 318 6184
ritz-carlton.com

The opulence of the Ritz-Carlton quietly asserts itself amidst the brash, trendy spots that dominate Dubai's beachfront and the hotel's spa is very much in keeping with the resort's general character. With treatments like Ritz's 24 carat gold massage, don't expect bargains here, but sheer delight, yes.

Map 3 A1 **Metro** Dubai Marina

Sanctuary Spa

04 377 2380

Pullman Dubai Mall Of The Emirates,
  Al Barsha 1

pullman-dubai.com

This compact spa sits in an enviable position on top of the Pullman hotel and, as all treatments come inclusive of access to the scenic rooftop swimming pool, it's worth arriving early to take a dip before the real pampering begins. Indoors, the facilities include a sauna, steam room and aquatherapy pool, and all treatments are carried out by highly skilled therapists.

Map 3 E3 **Metro** Mall Of The Emirates

Nail Bars

You are never too far from a perfect pedi in Dubai – the city's nail bars are pampering havens where you can enjoy basic treatments and massages in style. You will find at least one nail bar in each of the malls, and popular salons NStyle Nail Lounge (nstyleintl.com) and N.Bar (thegroomingco.com) have several locations. Also try The Organic Glow Beauty Lounge (04 434 3017, organicglowuae.com) and Tips & Toes (tipsntoeshaven.com).

Saray Spa

04 319 4630

Dubai Marriott Harbour
  Hotel & Suites,
  Dubai Marina

marriott.com

Taking its name from the caravanserais of the ancient Silk Route, the Saray Spa offers an Arabian-inspired experience. The spa's signature product range features natural and traditionally used elements from around the region including lemon, coffee, mint, frankincense, honey, rose, pomegranate and dates, as well as Dead Sea salts and mud. In addition to signature treatments, you could also opt for a more conventional Swedish massage or try the traditional hammam experience.

Map 3 B1 **Metro** Dubai Marina

SensAsia Urban Spa

04 349 8850
sensasiaspas.com

The Village, Jumeira 1

SensAsia is one of the most popular spas among Dubai expats and it's not hard to see why. The quality of service is excellent, the therapists well-trained and which ever branch you choose to visit, the treatments delivered in a gorgeous Asian-inspired setting. The emphasis is on Balinese and Thai-style treatments, although Elemis and Eve Lom facials are also available. In addition to this venue in Jumeira, other branches are located in Palm Jumeirah (04 422 7115) and Emirates Golf Club (04 417 9820) – the latter also has a menu of treatments designed specifically for golfers. Elsewhere, SensAsia Express (04 354 9228) caters to weary shoppers in need of rejuvenation at Mall Of The Emirates.

Map 1 H2 **Metro** Al Jafiliya

The Spa At Hilton Dubai Jumeirah

04 318 2406
hilton.com

Hilton Dubai Jumeirah Resort, Dubai Marina

Hilton Jumeirah's spa may not be the most glamorous in town, but the treatments can't be faulted – be it a facial, massage or slimming treatment you're after. Perched above the hustle and bustle of the JBR beach, the spa also features a nice relaxation area overlooking the bay.

Map 3 A1 **Metro** Jumeirah Lakes Towers

The Spa At Shangri-La

04 405 2441
Shangri-La Hotel, Trade Centre 1   shangri-la.com

This spa offers a holistic approach to healing, featuring traditional Asian treatments. The relaxation facilities are extensive, with a salon, barber, juice bar and boutique; the minimalist surroundings and the communal areas lean more towards fitness club than spa.

Map 2 C1 **Metro** Financial Centre

Spa At The Address Downtown Dubai

04 436 8888
The Address Downtown Dubai,
Downtown Dubai   theaddress.com

You step into total relaxation the moment you arrive at this spa, thanks to muted decor, ambient music, and a refreshing drink on arrival. The Spa has five treatment rooms for women, four for men, a couple's room, and a range of treatments including facials, massages and wraps using ESPA products. The spas at The Address Dubai Mall (04 438 8888) and The Address Dubai Marina (p.76) offer a similar experience.

Map 2 B3 **Metro** Burj Khalifa/Dubai Mall

Talise Spa

04 366 6818
Madinat Jumeirah, Al Sufouh 1   madinatjumeirah.com

This regal spa is made up of luxurious lounges and treatment rooms connected by garden walkways. The focus of the treatments is on natural therapies and the lovely facilities include a steam room, sauna and plunge pools.

Map 3 E1 **Metro** Mall Of The Emirates

Oriental hammam

Shopping

With souks, boutiques and mammoth malls at every turn, you won't have any problems spending your holiday money in Dubai.

Dubai provides many opportunities to indulge in a shopping spree: it is either a shopaholic's dream or nightmare, depending on who's paying the bill. Dubai's malls (p.200) are gleaming hubs of trade filled with a mix of international high-street brands and designer names. Most people head to the malls as their first stop, but it is also worth checking out some of Dubai's independent shops (p.217).

Practicality plays a large part in mall culture, and during the hotter months the malls are oases of cool in the sweltering city – somewhere to walk, shop, eat and be entertained – where you can escape the soaring heat for a few hours. From the smaller community shopping centres to the mega malls that have changed the skyline, shopping opportunities are everywhere. And with most shops open until at least 22:00 every night, and some until midnight at the weekends, there's plenty of time to browse. The popularity of the malls is evident from the crowds that they pull, particularly at the weekends, and it takes a dedicated shopper to tackle them on a Friday evening.

Souks (p.192) provide a slightly more original way to shop; they often hold a broad range of items, including souvenirs and traditional gifts, and you are able to bargain with traders to get a good price.

Saks Fifth Avenue

While prices for most items are comparable to elsewhere in the world, there are not many places that can beat Dubai's range and frequency of sales.

There are several places to buy carpets (p.187) and gold jewellery (p.188), but you'll need to bargain hard to get a good price. Electronics can be cheaper than they are in the UK or the US, and Dubai is the world's leading re-exporter of gold. For most items, there is enough choice to find something to fit any budget, from the streets of Karama (p.130) with its fake designer goods, to the shops in the malls (p.200) that sell the real thing. For the lowdown on where to find your essential Dubai buys, see p.186.

Sizing

Figuring out your size is fairly straightforward. International sizes are often printed on garment labels or the store will usually have a conversion chart on display. Otherwise, a UK size is always two higher than a US size (so a UK 10 is a US 6). To convert European sizes into US sizes, subtract 32 (so a European 38 is actually a US 6). To convert European sizes into UK sizes, a 38 is roughly a 10. As for shoes, a woman's UK 6 is a European 39 or US 8.5 and a men's UK 10 is a European 44 or a US 10.5.

Bargaining

Bargaining is still common practice in the souks and shopping areas of the UAE; you'll need to give it a go to get the best prices. Before you take the plunge, try to get an idea of prices from a few shops, as there can often be a significant difference. Once you've decided how much you are willing to spend, offer an initial bid that is roughly around half that price. Stay laidback and vaguely disinterested. When your initial offer is rejected (and it will be), keep going until you reach an agreement or until you have reached your limit. If the price isn't right, say so and walk out – the vendor will often follow and suggest a compromise price. The more you buy, the better the discount. When the price is agreed, it is considered bad form to back out of the sale.

While common in souks, bargaining isn't commonly accepted in malls and independent shops. However, use your discretion, as some shops such as jewellery stores, smaller electronics stores and eyewear optical centres do operate a set discount system and the price shown may be 'before discount'. Ask whether there is a discount on the marked price and you may end up with a bargain.

Shipping

The large number of international and local shipping and courier agencies makes transporting anything from a coffee pot to a car feasible. Both air and sea freight are available; air freight is faster but more expensive and not really suitable for large or heavy objects, whereas sea freight may take several weeks to arrive but it is cheaper and, as it is possible to rent containers, size and weight are not as much of an issue. With so many companies to choose from, it is worth getting a few quotes and finding out what will happen when the goods arrive; some offer no services at the destination while others, usually the bigger ones, will clear customs and deliver right to the door. For smaller items, or those that have to be delivered quickly, air freight is better, and the items can be tracked. Empost (600 56 5555) offers both local and international courier and air freight services at competitive prices.

Mall Eats

Dubai has some fantastic cafes and restaurants in its malls. The Lime Tree Café & Kitchen (p.273) at Ibn Battuta Mall, Aprés (p.251) and Almaz by Momo at Mall Of The Emirates, Organic Foods & Cafe in The Dubai Mall and More Café (04 284 3805, morecafe.biz) at Mirdif City Centre should get you ready for more retail.

Art

The art scene in Dubai, quiet for so long, has been enjoying rapid growth over the past few years. There are galleries and exhibitions displaying traditional and contemporary art by Arabic and international artists working in a range of media. The Majlis Gallery (04 353 6233, themajlisgallery.com), located in a traditional windtower house, is a great venue for fine art, hand-made glass, pottery and other unusual pieces. For cutting edge art, check out Opera Gallery (04 323 0909, operagallery.com) or XVA Gallery (04 353 5383, xvagallery.com), while Art Source (04 285 6972, theartsource. ae) in Rashidiya stocks a range of original artwork – a framing service is also offered. You can find information on art auctions, as well as art fairs and gallery openings at artinthecity.com.

Souk Madinat Jumeirah has the largest concentration of boutiques selling art, glass and photographs, both originals and reproductions. Many of the galleries and showrooms have a framing service or can recommend one. There are some excellent framing shops on Plant Street in Satwa (Map 1 N4) and in Karama Market (Map 5 A4).

An Arabian Shopping Experience

There are a few places in Dubai where you can sidestep the glitzy mall experience and enjoy more authentic Arabian-style shopping. The Bastakiya area has a bohemian vibe and its narrow walkways, traditional windtowers and courtyards provide the perfect setting for the Bastaflea market. Souk Madinat Jumeirah's (p.197) walkways are a great place to shop for jewellery, photography and art in various mediums, while Souk Al Bahar (p.197) has some quirky boutiques and furniture stores selling traditional items. Wafi's underground marketplace, Khan Murjan (p.196), houses 150 stalls underneath its spectacular stained glass ceiling. Trade Routes, inside Dubai Festival City (p.202), is another modern take on traditional Arabian souks. Each area holds a broad range of shops as well as several restaurants should you need to refuel after you shop.

Carpets

Carpets are one of the region's signature items, although they tend to be imported from Iran, Turkey and Pakistan. The price of a piece depends on a number of factors: its origin, the material used, the number of knots, and whether or not it is hand-made. The

Fake Goods

The consumer protection department of the Dubai Department of Economic Development (dubaided. gov.ae) has launched a crackdown on the sale of counterfeit goods; however, the sale of such items is still very common in Dubai. If it has a logo, then you'll be able to find a 'genuine copy' version of it in Karama (p.130). The quality of goods varies, with some items being almost indistinguishable from the originals, and others being hilariously bad imitations. Inspect items properly to ensure you are buying the genuine article and not a very good fake.

most expensive carpets are usually those hand-made with silk in Iran. The higher the quality, the neater the back, so turn the carpets over – if the pattern is clearly depicted and the knots are all neat, the carpet is of higher quality than those that are indistinct. Try to do some research so that you have a basic idea of what you are looking for before you go, just in case you happen to meet an unscrupulous carpet dealer. Fortunately, most will happily explain the differences between the rugs and share their extensive knowledge.

Ask to see a selection of various carpets and get a feel for the differences between hand-made or machine-made silk, wool or blend carpets. Prices range from a few hundred to tens of thousands of dirhams. It is always worth bargaining to get a better price. To find the perfect piece, head to Fabindia (Al Mankhool Road, Bur Dubai, 04 398 9633), the Pride of Kashmir (04 368 6110) in Souk Madinat Jumeirah (p.197) and Mercato (p.208), or Persian Carpet House (04 330 3277) in the Emirates Towers. There's also a good collection of places in Deira – National Iranian Carpets (04 221 9800) and Kashmir Gallery (04 222 5271) – and in Souk Al Bahar (p.197) in Downtown Dubai.

Gold

Gold is notably cheaper in the UAE than in Europe, making it a popular souvenir and a main attraction for many visitors. Dubai is the world's leading re-exporter of gold and you'll find a jeweller in even the smallest of malls. It is available in 18, 21, 22 and 24 carats and is sold according to the international gold rate. This means that, for an identical piece, whether you buy it in Mall Of The Emirates (p.207) or in the Gold Souk (p.194), there should be very little difference in price. You should do your research before buying anything though, especially if you decide to get a piece custom-made to a design, such as a necklace with your name in Arabic. Of course, don't forget to bargain.

Many of the world's finest jewellery stores have outlets in Dubai. Both Cartier and Tiffany have numerous branches thoughout the city. Simply asking for a discount, even in these upmarket retailers, can get good results. You'll find a large selection of outlets, most of which are open to bargaining, in the Gold & Diamond Park (04 347 7788) at Interchange 4 on Sheikh Zayed Road, and this venue offers a slightly cooler, less frenetic shopping experience than the Gold Souk.

Souvenirs

There is the usual selection of tacky souvenirs available in Dubai, but an equally impressive range of tasteful items are much more worthy of your money. Hand-carved wooden trinket boxes, sometimes filled with traditional oudh (a kind of incense) are popular, as are beaded wall hangings from the Textile Souk (p.199), khanjars (traditional Arabic daggers), pashminas and keffiyeh headscarves, embroidered slippers, hand-woven carpets and shisha pipes. For the ultimate in Arabian kitsch, pick up a gaudy mosque alarm clock that wakes you up with the sound of the call to prayer – it won't win you any style awards, but you'll probably be the only person on your street that has one. Good places to hunt for souvenirs include Souk Madinat Jumeirah (p.197) and Karama (p.130).

Tailoring

If you're in town for longer than a few days, it is a great opportunity to get some garments made. Tailors can be found in most areas, but the area around Dubai Museum (p.87) in Bur Dubai, or Plant Street in Satwa (p.130), are good places to start. A good tailor will be able to make a garment from scratch (rather than just make alterations), either from a photo or diagram, or by copying an existing item. If they don't get the garment spot on, they will happily make the necessary alterations. Allow one week or more to make sure you don't run out of time for alterations after the first fitting.

Dream Girl Tailors (04 349 5445) in Satwa has a huge following; it is great for everything from taking up trousers to making ball gowns. Skirts cost around Dhs.60 and dresses from around Dhs.150, depending on the complexity of the pattern. Dream Boy (04 352 1840), in Meena Bazaar, is good for shirts and suits, as is Whistle and Flute (04 342 9229); shirts usually start from Dhs.85 and suits from around Dhs.1,000. One of Dubai's most highly regarded tailors is Kachins (04 352 1386), where you may pay a little extra for a suit or shirt, but the fabric and cut will be worth it. Santoba Tailors (04 393 1234), near Choithram in Meena Bazaar, is another great option. Its tailors will design, copy, or alter suits, dresses and anything else you can think up – it specialises in European designs and slick shirts and suits.

Clockwise from top left: Al Faheidi Street, Karama Market, 2nd Of December Road

Souks & Markets

If you want to add a slice of cultural indulgence to your shopping list, head to the souks where you'll find bargains amid the bustle.

There are a number of souks and markets in Dubai. The souks are the traditional trading areas, some more formally demarcated than others. In keeping with tradition, bargaining is expected and cash gives the best leverage.

The Gold, Spice and Textile Souks line either side of the creek, but parking is limited, so if possible it is better to go to these areas by taxi or, if you are visiting all three, park on one side of the creek and take an abra (p.65) to the other side.

Western-style markets are becoming more popular: they are usually based around crafts and are often seasonal. The Covent Garden Market (p.193) is set up along The Walk, JBR, during the cooler months. Another street market can be found along the pedestrian promenade outside the Dubai Marina Mall. Both are great launch pads for local talents, with artists, jewellers and other crafty types displaying their wares.

Global Village (globalvillage.ae), on the Emirates Road near Arabian Ranches (Map 1 E9), is a huge collection of stalls, food and entertainment from all over the world. It runs from November to February and is a good spot to pick up everything from Chinese lanterns to honey from Yemen. Organised by country, you can spend hours exploring the wares before enjoying a unique range of dishes in the international foodcourt. Just don't overdo dinner before getting on the fairground rides. Global Village is open from16:00 to midnight, Saturday to Wednesday, and until 01:00 on Thursday and Friday. Entrance costs Dhs.10 and is free for children under 3 years old.

Covent Garden Market

The vibrancy of this street market comes from its street entertainers, open stalls and morning strollers along Jumeirah Beach Residence's cobbled beachfront promenade. You can pick up canvas or watercolour paintings from emerging artists for a rock-bottom price. You will also find stalls selling fashion items, hand-made jewellery, confectionery and kids' toys. The market is located in the Rimal sector of The Walk, Jumeirah Beach Residence on Wednesdays and Thursdays 17:00 till midnight and Fridays and Saturdays 10:00 to 21:00.
Map 3 A1 **Metro** Dubai Marina

Dubai Flea Market

This flea market is a great place to take advantage of Dubai's transient population. As people pack up and move on, an escapee's excess baggage could become a bargain hunter's treasure. For the Dhs.3 entry fee into Safa Park or Dhs.5 fee into Uptown Mirdif, you can peruse the stalls covered with furniture, books, clothing and a broad range of unwanted items and home-made crafts. The Dubai Flea Market (dubai-fleamarket.com) is set up on the first Saturday of every month at Safa Park and every third Saturday at Uptown Mirdif. Another market, the Dubai Designer Market

(dubaidesignermarket.com), takes place on the second Saturday of every month in the Sky Bubble – Meydan. It is free to enter and you can pick up genuine second-hand luxury goods – check the website for the schedule.
Map 2 A1 **Metro** Business Bay

Electronics Souk

At the heart of Bur Dubai's traditional shopping area, and bordering the Textile Souk (p.199), Al Fahidi Street is home to Dubai's electronics souk. A great place to wander round in the cooler evenings, it's perfect for a bit of local colour and some great shopping. This area is always busy but it really comes to life at night – if you're unsure whether you're in the right place, just head for the neon lights. Prices are negotiable and competitive but the vendors know the value of what they're selling. Don't make your purchases at the first shop you go into; rather, take the time to look around at the range and prices available. Although goods are often cheaper here, if you are making a big purchase, it may be worth paying that bit extra at a major retailer, so that you have more security if something goes wrong. **Map** 4 C2 **Metro** Al Ghubaiba

Gold Souk

This is Dubai's best-known souk and a must-do for every visitor. In addition to being an exotic experience to remember, the souk is a good place to buy customised jewellery for unique souvenirs and gifts at a reasonable price.

On the Deira side of the creek, the meandering lanes are lined with shops selling gold, silver, pearls and precious stones. These can be bought as they are, or in a variety of settings so this is definitely a place to try your bargaining skills – let the vendor offer you the best discount to get the ball rolling. Gold is sold by weight according to the daily international price and so will be much the same as in the shops in malls – the price of the workmanship is where you will have more bargaining power. Most of the outlets operate split shifts, so try not to visit between 13:00 and 16:00 as many will be closed. The Gold Souk is shaded so visiting during the hotter daytime hours is an option, but there is added sparkle when you visit in the evenings as the lights reflect on the gold and gems. **Map** 4 C2 **Metro** Al Ras

Karama Complex

Karama is one of the older residential districts in Dubai, and it has a big shopping area that is one of the best places to find a bargain. The best spot is the Karama Complex, a long street running through the middle of the district that is lined by shops on both sides. The area is best known for bargain clothing, sports goods, gifts and souvenirs, and it is notorious for being the hotbed of counterfeit items in Dubai. As you wander round, you will be offered 'copy watches, copy bags' with every step, and if you show any interest you will be whisked into a back room to view the goods. If you're not interested, a simple 'no thank you' will suffice, or even just ignore the vendor completely – it may seem rude, but sometimes it's the only way to cope with the incessant invitations to view counterfeit items. Two of the most popular shops are Blue Marine and Green Eye, while the imaginatively named Asda is around the corner, and offers high quality handbags and accessories crammed into two floors. It's pretty claustrophobic but the range is excellent.

There's a huge range of T-shirts, shoes, shorts and sunglasses at very reasonable prices in Karama. There are several shops selling gifts and souvenirs, from toy camels to mosque alarm clocks and stuffed scorpions to pashminas. Gifts Tent (04 335 4416) is one of the larger outlets and has a wide range, including every colour of pashmina imaginable. The salesmen are happy to take most of them out so you can find exactly the right shade. With loads of small, inexpensive restaurants serving a range of cuisines, you won't go hungry while pounding the streets of Karama. Try Chef Lanka (04 335 3050), Aryaas (04 335 5776) or Saravana Bhavan (p.288).
Map 4 B3 **Metro** Al Karama

Khan Murjan

For something a little different, head to Wafi's underground souk. Khan Murjan's magnificent stained glass ceiling (which stretches 64 metres) and long curved arches help make this an atmospheric place to shop. The souk features over 150 stalls selling jewellery, antiques, Arabic perfumes and souvenirs. It is particularly good if you wish to spice up your home with traditional arts and crafts; there are workshops where artisans can create various bits of arts and crafts on site. In the centre of the souk, you'll find an open air marble courtyard and the Khan Murjan Restaurant (04 327 9795), which serves pan-Arabic culinary treats.
Map 4 B5 **Metro** Healthcare City

Souk Al Bahar

While this isn't a souk in the conventional sense, Souk Al Bahar, in Downtown Dubai, is a modern take on the concept: similar to the souk at Madinat Jumeirah (p.71), the Arabian-style mall features dimly lit corridors, carved wood and a small range of shops. Compared to the retail extravaganza of the adjacent Dubai Mall (p.204), Souk Al Bahar is unlikely to set a serious shopper's pulse racing but the atmospheric setting makes for a fun experience – not to mention excellent photo opportunities. It's also a good spot to stock up on souvenirs. Stop by at Fortix (04 420 3680) for small gifts to bring home, or try Pride of Kashmir (04 420 3606) to bag an exotic rug. For unique household items, Marina Exotic Home Interiors (04 420 0191) carries a range of home decoration pieces with a distinct regional flair.

The main reason for turning up at Souk Al Bahar is the centre's vibrant bar and dining scene. New York favourite Dean & Deluca (04 420 0336) is a safe bet for breakfast, light bites and coffee, while Margaux (p.276) offers Mediterranean-inspired light bites and gorgeous views. Once darkness falls, there are several bars for a post-shop cool down.

Map 2 B3 **Metro** Burj Khalifa/Dubai Mall

Souk Madinat Jumeirah

Souk Madinat Jumeirah is a recreation of a traditional souk, complete with narrow alleyways, authentic architecture and motorised abras. The blend of outlets is unlike anywhere else in Dubai, with boutique shops, galleries, cafes, restaurants and bars. The layout can be a little confusing; there are maps throughout and the main features are signposted. If you're really lost, staff will happily direct you. The souk is home to a concentration of art boutiques, including Gallery One which sells photos with a local flavour (04 368 6055) and Spirit of Art Gallery (04 368 6207). The stalls in the outside areas sell souvenirs, some tasteful and some tacky. For holiday clobber, eye-catching but expensive swimming gear can be found at Vilebrequin (04 368 6531), Via Rodeo (04 368 6568) and Tommy Bahama (04 368 6031).

There are more than 20 waterfront cafes, bars and restaurants to choose from, including some of Dubai's hottest night spots: Jambase (p.312) and Barzar (p.304) are among the popular choices around here, to name a few. There's also the impressive Madinat Theatre (madinattheatre.com) which sees international and regional artists perform everything from ballet to comedy.
Map 3 E1 **Metro** Mall Of The Emirates

Spice Souk

With its narrow streets and exotic aromas, a wander through the Spice Souk, next to the Gold Souk, is a great way to get a feel for the way the city used to be. Most of the stalls sell the same ranges and the vendors are usually happy to advise on the types of spices and their uses. This is a good spot to pick up an exotic souvenir or two – you may even be able to pick up some saffron at a bargain price. The shops operate split shifts, but there is more bustle in the evenings. Friday is not the best day to visit as many of the shops are closed until the evening. **Map** 4 C2 **Metro** Al Ras

Textile Souk

Textile Souk

The Textile Souk in Bur Dubai is stocked with every fabric and colour imaginable. Textiles are imported from all over the world, with many of the more elaborate coming from the Indian subcontinent and the Far East. There are silks and satins in an amazing array of colours and patterns, velvets and intricately embroidered fabrics. Basic cottons can sometimes be harder to find but you can always try Satwa. Prices are negotiable and there are often sales, particularly around the major holidays of Eid and Diwali, and the shopping festivals. It is worth having a look in a few shops before parting with your cash as stock and prices vary considerably. The mornings tend to be a more relaxed time to browse.

Nearby, Meena Bazaar is the area that most taxi drivers head for if you ask for the Textile Souk. It has an impressive number of fabric stores. Rivoli Textiles (04 335 0075) has a good selection. Be sure to haggle. **Map** 4 C2 **Metro** Al Ghubaiba

Shopping Malls

More than merely shopping destinations, Dubai's malls are epicentres of activity, with eating, drinking and even skiing on offer.

BurJuman

04 352 0222
burjuman.com

Sheikh Khalifa Bin Zayed Rd, Al Mankhool

One of Dubai's original shopping havens, BurJuman is renowned for its blend of designer and high-street labels attracting many a well-heeled shopper. The mall houses many famous brands, including Christian Dior, Gap, Escada and Just Cavalli, as well as some interesting smaller shops and legendary New York department store Saks Fifth Avenue. In addition to clothing and fashion, you can stock up on electronics, home decor and sports goods. There are also a few independent music shops that sell a good range of CDs and DVDs, and a branch of Virgin Megastore. The two foodcourts and numerous cafes are well arranged for people-watching, including the popular Pavillion Gardens on the third floor, and Paul on the ground floor, where you can dine outside during the cooler months. The mall can be accessed directly from the Dubai Metro and there is plenty of underground parking and a taxi rank just outside (this gets pretty congested after 18:00 and at weekends). Major renovation and expansion works are scheduled to run for up to two years starting from late 2011, but the mall should stay open. **Map** 4 B3 **Metro** BurJuman Center

BurJuman

Deira City Centre

Al Ittihad Rd, Port Saeed

04 295 1010
deiracitycentre.com

A stalwart of Dubai's mall scene, this centre attracts the most cosmopolitan crowd. The three floors offer a diverse range of shops where you can find anything from a postcard to a Persian carpet. There's an 11 screen cinema, a children's entertainment centre, a jewellery court, a textiles court and an area dedicated to local furniture, gifts and souvenirs.

It's all anchored by a huge Carrefour hypermarket, Paris Gallery and Debenhams, as well as trendy department store Iconic (p.215). In addition, many high-street brands are represented, including Gap, Warehouse, Topshop, Forever 21, Next and River Island. A number of designer boutiques can be found, mostly on the top floor. The City Gate section (on the same level as carparks P2 and P3) is dominated by electronics retailers.

The mall has two foodcourts: one on the first floor, next to Magic Planet, serving mainly fastfood, and one on the second floor, featuring several good sit-down restaurants. Thanks to the Deira City Centre Metro station, it is now easier to get to and from than before – which is great because the taxi queues can get very long, especially during weekends and in the evenings. **Map** 4 D5 **Metro** Deira City Centre

Dubai Festival City

Al Rebat St, Festival City

800 332
dubaifestivalcity.com

Dubai Festival City incorporates the Festival Centre and The Festival Waterfront Centre. The area features around 370 retail outlets (including 25 flagship stores) and more than 90 restaurants, including 40 alfresco dining options. The need for retail therapy can be sated by the broad range of fashion, electronics and homeware outlets spread over 2.9 million square feet of retail space. Brit favourite Marks & Spencer (04 206 6466) is among the big draws here, in addition to numerous high-street clothing labels. For the finer things in life, there is also a 25,000 square foot modern gold souk where you can peruse gold from all over the world.

It's not just shopping though; The Festival Waterfront Centre has dramatic water features and performance spaces to keep shoppers entertained. There is also a Grand Cinema (04 232 8328) and a 10 lane bowling alley on site. You can happily spend an entire day here, dining at Romano's Macaroni Grill (04 232 6001) before relaxing in the Belgian Beer Cafe (p.305). **Map** 1 J4 **Metro** Emirates

Dubai Marina Mall
04 436 1020
Off Shk Zayed Rd, Dubai Marina   dubaimarinamall.com
Located in Dubai Marina's thriving community, and within walking distance of the popular beachfront promenade in Jumeirah Beach Residence (p.104), this mall's 160 outlets offer a mix of plush designer goods and high-street regulars. Shops like New Look (04 399 7740), Reiss (04 399 7266), Karen Millen (04 399 7525), Ted Baker (04 399 7377) and Accessorize (04 399 7953) anchor the mall's offering of reasonably priced fashion. You can also pick up kids' items at Mamas and Papas (04 399 7807) or the Early Learning Centre (04 434 2642). If you get hungry while browsing, there are several restaurants and cafes. The large top-floor foodcourt features many of the

usual fastfood suspects. On the ground floor and mezzanine level, you'll find more varied options, with restaurants such as Carluccio's (04 399 7844), Gourmet Burger Kitchen (04 399 7705) and Yo! Sushi (04 399 7708) among the popular draws. Many of these restaurants also boast attractive alfresco areas along the water's edge. The Favourite Things Mother and Child play area (04 434 1984, favouritethings.com) provides plenty of entertainment for kids, and you can leave your kids there so they can enjoy supervised play while you shop. There is also a branch of Reel Cinemas (reelcinemas.ae) showing a selection of the latest releases. Yet to open is the Gourmet Tower, which will offer world-class cuisine with waterfront views. **Map** 3 A1 **Metro** Jumeirah Lakes Towers

The Dubai Mall

800 38224 6255

Nr Interchange 1, Financial Centre Rd,
 Downtown Dubai   thedubaimall.com

The Dubai Mall is one of the world's largest malls; it will eventually house over 1,200 stores, including 160 eateries. The huge shopping and entertainment complex houses an extensive range of stores, an Olympic size ice skating rink, a catwalk for fashion shows, an enormous aquarium, a 22 screen cinema, an indoor theme park called SEGA Republic (04 448 8484), a luxury hotel, and a children's edutainment centre called KidZania (kidzania.ae).

   The shopping highlights are manifold, but unique to Dubai Mall are the regional flagship stores for New York department store Bloomingdale's, French department store Galeries Lafayette (04 339 9933), the world-renowned

The Dubai Mall

toy shop Hamleys (04 339 8889) and UK upmarket food retailer Waitrose (04 434 0700). You'll find all of the haute couture designer brands along Fashion Avenue and there is a sprawling souk with 66 jewellery outlets. Inside the mall, touch-screen maps and knowledgeable staff make it easy to find what you are looking for. For a complete contrast, cross the wooden bridge over the Burj Khalifa Lake and you'll find yourself in Souk Al Bahar (p.197). The tranquillity of its dimly lit passageways offers a more relaxing stop after the onslaught of the mall.

Map 2 C3 **Metro** Burj Khalifa/Dubai Mall

Dubai Outlet Mall
04 423 4666

Dubai – Al Ain Rd (Route 66),
Dubailand
dubaioutletmall.com

In a city where the emphasis is on excess, it is refreshing to find a mall dedicated to saving money. Dubai's first 'outlet' mall may be quite a way out of town, along the Al Ain highway, but bargain hunters will find it's worth the drive. A wide range of luxury brands and designer labels are on offer at heavily discounted prices, in addition to a good selection of bargain sports goods and children's wear. **Map** 1 G7

Ibn Battuta Mall
04 362 1900

Off Sheikh Zayed Rd, The Gardens
ibnbattutamall.com

This mall is divided into six zones each based on a region that explorer Ibn Battuta visited in the 14th century. There are several anchor stores, including Debenhams (p.214) and Géant hypermarket (04 368 5880). Shops are loosely grouped:

China Court is dedicated to entertainment, with several restaurants and a 21 screen cinema, including the UAE's first IMAX screen. Nearby is Sharaf DG (04 368 5115), and iStyle (04 366 9797) for fans of Apple products; it also does repairs in case you dropped your iPod into the hotel pool.

The fashion conscious should head to India Court for the likes of Forever 21 (04 368 5232), H&M (04 364 9819), River Island (04 368 5961), Topshop (04 368 5948) and popular independent boutique Ginger & Lace (04 368 5109). Persia Court is designed as the lifestyle area, anchored by Debenhams (04 368 5282). The foodcourts are at either end of the mall. To reward the kids for trailing round after you, there's a Fun City in Tunisia Court. The taxi points are by the entrance to each court. **Map** 1 B2 **Metro** Ibn Battuta Mall

Mall Of The Emirates

04 409 9000

Sheikh Zayed Rd, Al Barsha 1   malloftheemirates.com

Mall Of The Emirates is more than a mall, it's a lifestyle destination. It houses an indoor ski slope (Ski Dubai, p.156), the Kempinski Mall of the Emirates Hotel, the Pullman Dubai Mall of the Emirates and the Dubai Community Theatre & Arts Centre (p.230). There are more than 500 outlets selling everything from forks to high fashion. The mall has been extended to include the Fashion Dome which features a selection of restaurants and fashion outlets including a branch of More Café (04 395 0967), a Boutique 1 store and Sephora – there are also plenty of designer names. The mall is anchored by Carrefour hypermarket, Dubai's largest branch of Debenhams (p.214), Harvey Nichols (p.214) and

Centrepoint, which is home to Babyshop, Home Centre, Lifestyle, Shoe Mart and Splash. There is also a VOX Cinema (04 341 4222) where you can enjoy a film in Gold Class, which means enormous leather armchairs and waiter service throughout. Nearby, the sizeable Magic Planet (800 386) includes a bowling alley, and a myriad of games and rides. Label devotees should head for Rodeo Drive (04 340 0347) to get their fix of designer labels such as Burberry, Dolce & Gabanna, Salvatore Ferragamo, Tod's and Versace. If you're more into street chic, there are two H&M stores, a branch of Reiss (04 341 0515), and a large Zara (04 341 3171). Those looking for accessories and jewellery will love Boom & Mellow (04 341 3993). Sporty types should head straight to GO Sports (04 341 3251) for all-season apparel. For entertainment, Virgin Megastore (04 341 4353) has a bookshop and many international magazines alongside CDs, DVDs, mobile phones and computers.

You'll need to keep your energy up to explore this large mall so it's fortunate there is a wide range of dining options, from the Swiss chalet feel of Après (p.251) to a large selection of cafes and two foodcourts. Several taxis queue up outside and you can also access the Metro directly from the mall. **Map** 3 E2 **Metro** Mall Of The Emirates

Mercato
04 344 4161

Jumeira Rd, Jumeira 1 · mercatoshoppingmall.com

Mercato is the largest mall in Jumeira, with more than 90 shops, restaurants, cafes and a cinema. As you drive along Jumeira Road, the renaissance-style architecture really makes

Mercato stand out, and, once inside, the huge glass roof provides natural light and enhances the Mediterranean feel.

The mall is anchored by a large Spinneys supermarket (04 349 6900), a Virgin Megastore (04 344 6971) and Gap (04 342 0745). There is a good mix of designer boutiques and high-street brands in the mall, and shops range from the reasonably priced Pull and Bear (04 344 7214) to the more exclusive Hugo Boss (04 342 2021). For everyday fashions and holiday essentials, try Topshop (04 344 2677), Massimo Dutti (04 344 7124) and Mango (04 344 7184).

There is a foodcourt and a number of cafes and restaurants, including French cafe Paul (04 349 9115) and Bella Donna (04 344 7701), an Italian restaurant where you can dine alfresco. The cinema and large Fun City play area (04 349 9976) should keep most of the family occupied.
Map 1 G2 **Metro** Financial Centre

Mirdif City Centre

800 6422

Emirates Rd & Tripoli St, Mirdif   mirdifcitycentre.com

What makes this mall stand out from the rest? Its bright, modern interior, its mix of high-street and designer brands, and a good few stores that don't have presence elsewhere in Dubai. The mall's highlights include large branches of Boutique 1, Debenhams, Carrefour and Topshop, as well as Dubai debutants Pottery Barn and American Eagle Outfitters. If you have kids in tow, entertainment comes in the form of Playnation (playnationme.com), which is an emporium of fun times with highlights that include an indoor skydiving centre, a water-themed play centre, a 10 pin bowling alley, an edutainment centre and an arcade. Top it off with a branch of More Cafe, a large carpark and well-stocked foodcourts, and this is definitely one to visit if you fancy moseying down to Mirdif or are staying with friends or relatives based in this part of town. **Map** 1 K5 **Metro** Rashidiya

The Walk, Jumeirah Beach Residence   04 390 0091

Jumeirah Beach Residence, Dubai Marina

While this isn't strictly a mall, and the selection is rather limited, The Walk is great for browsing and cafe culture. It is a fully pedestrianised shopping area that stretches 1.7 kilometres along the beachfront. Outlets are located either on the ground level or on the plaza level of six clusters of towers called Murjan, Sadaf, Bahar, Rimal, Amwaj and Shams. The plaza level of each cluster can be accessed from large staircases, or by the lifts at ground level and in the carpark. The largest cluster of shops is concentrated at the Murjan end of the strip. Fashion favourite Boutique 1 (04 425 7888) is located here. The Style Outlet has taken over the section that used to be occupied by Saks Fifth Avenue, and now carries discounted designer clothing – to the delight of fashion-conscious bargain hunters. In the afternoons, people congregate in the many cafes in the area – particularly popular are Le Pain Quotidien (04 437 0141) and Paul (04 437 6494), and there are plenty of alfresco restaurants to dine in come the evening. Parking is available along the beach near Bahar, or in designated areas of the Murjan carpark. Most of the shops open at 10:00 and close at 22:00.
Map 3 A1 **Metro** Dubai Marina

Wafi

04 324 4555
wafi.com

Oud Metha Rd, Umm Hurair

Wafi is one of Dubai's most exclusive malls and a popular stop for the Big Bus Tours (p.145). The store directory reads like a who's who in design, with a wide range of international labels available to splurge on should you have some holiday cash burning a hole in your pocket. Among some of the mall's most interesting boutique is Ginger & Lace (04 324 5699) which stocks a mix of funky fashion styles. Alternatively, you could head out to the top-end department store Salam (04 704 8484) to quench your thirst for all manner of designer gear under one roof. For a break from the upper echelons of fashion, there's also a large Marks & Spencer (04 324 5145), offering tried and tested high-street styles and clothing staples from the UK.

The Khan Murjan (p.196) souk houses over 150 shops selling antiques, jewellery and souvenirs in an atmospheric setting. Shopping aside, there are a number of cafes and restaurants in the mall, including Italian restaurant Biella (04 324 4666), where you can eat in the alfresco dining area. Wafi Gourmet (04 324 4433) is a great place to pick up freshly made Arabic dishes and a delicious selection of olives and dates.

The children's entertainment area, Encounter Zone (04 324 7747), is very popular and has age-specific attractions. If you feel the need for pampering, or an evening out, head across to the Pyramids complex where there are some excellent bars and restaurants and a renowned spa (p.172).

Map 4 B5 **Metro** Healthcare City

Wafi

Department Stores

The scope of department stores covers the full shopping spectrum, from the epitome of chic at Saks Fifth Avenue to the functionality of M&S.

Debenhams

04 340 7575

Mall Of The Emirates, Al Barsha · debenhams.com

A stalwart of the British high street, Debenhams has five stores in Dubai: Deira City Centre (p.202), Ibn Battuta Mall (p.206), Mall of the Emirates (p.207), Mirdif City Centre (p.210) and The Dubai Mall (p.204). The branches all stock perfumes and cosmetics, clothing and homewares. They carry the popular Designers at Debenhams range with diffusion lines from John Rocha, Betty Jackson, Jasper Conran, Matthew Williamson and Ben de Lisi. **Map** 3 E2 **Metro** Mall Of The Emirates

Harvey Nichols

04 409 8888

Mall Of The Emirates, Al Barsha 1 · harveynichols.com

Dubai simply couldn't call itself a luxury destination without its own Harvey Nichols (the largest branch outside the UK). It contains a large selection of high-rolling fashion, food, beauty and homeware brands, as well as an intimidating selection of sunglasses. Pick up fashion treats from Jimmy Choo, Diane Von Furstenberg, Juicy Couture, Hermes and Sergio Rossi, then head to the top floor for the popular Almaz by Momo (04 409 8877), a restaurant, juice bar and shisha cafe all in one. **Map** 3 E2 **Metro** Mall Of The Emirates

Iconic

04 294 3444

Deira City Centre, Port Saeed landmarkgroup.com

This store screams urban style and youthful designs – all 70,000 square feet of it. Hidden away at one end of Deira City Centre (you can find it by the Metro entrance) the store stocks high-street and designer fashion for men and women from an assortment of international brand names. It also has an electronics boutique, accessories section, cosmetics area and two restaurants. **Map** 4 D5 **Metro** Deira City Centre

Jashanmal

04 232 9023

Festival Centre, Festival City jashanmalgroup.com

One of Dubai's original department stores, Jashanmal is the importer for several brands including Burberry, Clarks shoes and Mexx. With books, cameras, fashion, gifts, homeware, kitchen appliances and luggage on offer, the stores are definitely worth a look. The new Festival City concept store also houses a 'Cook and Coffee' lifestyle section, where cooking demonstrations will take place, and the other branches are set to follow suit. **Map** 1 J4 **Metro** Emirates

Marks & Spencer

04 206 6466

Festival Centre, Festival City marksandspencerme.com

One of the best known brands in the UK, M&S sells men's, women's and children's clothes and shoes, along with a small selection of food. It is famous for its underwear selection and has a reputation for quality. You'll also find more fashion-forward lines including Limited Collection, Per Una, and Autograph alongside the traditional styles it has been carrying for years. The brand new flagship store is located in Mall Of The Emirates (p.207), while other branches are located in Wafi (p.212), Deira City Centre (p.202) and The Dubai Mall (p.204). **Map** 1 J4 **Metro** Emirates

Saks Fifth Avenue
04 351 5551
BurJuman, Al Mankhool   saksfifthavenue.com

Anchoring the extension to BurJuman is the second-largest Saks Fifth Avenue outside the US. The name is synonymous with style, elegance, and the good life, encapsulated on two floors of paradise for the label conscious. You'll find designers galore, including Christian Dior, Jean Paul Gaultier, Prada, Agent Provocateur and Tiffany & Co, in addition to a personalised shopping service.

Map 4 B3 **Metro** BurJuman Center

Supermarkets & Hypermarkets

The city's large supermarkets and hypermarkets stock a good range of international products and a comprehensive range of electronics, household goods, luggage and mobile phones. Carrefour (carrefouruae.com) has several locations in the city, and it is the best place to buy French products (particularly good are its crusty bread and selection of French cheeses). Its stores also stock camping gear, clothes, music, DVDs and stationery. UK store Waitrose has branches in Dubai Marina Mall (04 434 2624) and The Dubai Mall (04 434 0700) and its deli counter is great for picnic items and snacks. Spinneys (spinneys-dubai.com) stocks a great range of imported food items.

Ibn Battuta Mall

Independent & Noteworthy Shops

Dubai's independent scene has improved greatly in recent years. You'll find the odd store in Souk Al Bahar (p.197) or The Walk, Jumeirah Beach Residence (p.104), but Jumeira Road in Jumeira is one of the most popular destinations; in addition to individual stores in converted villas, the local malls here are fruitful grounds to hunt for unique items and hard-to-find brands.

Fabindia (04 398 9633, fabindia.com) has one of only two branches outside India in Dubai. A riot of bright colours and subtle hues, the clothing ranges for men and women

combine Indian and western styles. The hand-crafted fabrics, including soft furnishings, table cloths and cushion covers, will add an ethnic touch to your home. Similar in style, Mumbai Se carries a range of funky fashions and home decoration pieces by modern Indian designers at its stores in BurJuman (p.200), The Dubai Mall (p.204), Dubai Marina Mall (p.203) and Festival Centre (p.202). Elsewhere, fashion boutique S*uce stocks a range of funky accessories, quirky fashions and gifts at its eclectic boutiques in The Village Mall (04 344 7270) and The Dubai Mall (04 339 9696). Fans of designer labels can head out to Boutique 1 on The Walk in JBR (04 425 7888); a bigger branch is located in Mall Of The Emirates (04 395 1200). Those looking for home accessories should consider Marina Exotic Home Interiors. The Mall Of The Emirates branch (04 341 0314) carries a great range of homewares with distinct regional flair: think colourful cushions, lanterns and elaborate wood carvings. Burlesque (04 346 1616) on Al Wasl Road is an elaborate store with highly romantic furniture and plenty of floral prints. This is the place to head if you are bored with formulaic approaches to interior design and would like some

Gold & Diamonds

The Gold & Diamond Park (04 347 7788, goldanddiamondpark. com), is a great place to buy jewellery if you are more interested in buying than enjoying the souk experience. There are branches of many of the outlets that are also found in the Gold Souk (p.194) but here they are much quieter (Map 5 C2).

stylish, but eccentric, pieces to take home. Should you be in the market for something more substantial, Pinky Furniture & Novelties (04 422 1720, pinkyfurnitureuae.com) is particularly good for buying Indian teak furniture. The warehouse shop is located in Al Barsha. For home decoration that's easier to carry with you, look no further than Gallery One: this specialist shop carries contemporary, beautifully framed Arabian prints and photography. There are several branches across town, including stores in Mall Of The Emirates (04 341 4488), Souk Madinat Jumeirah (04 368 6055) and The Walk, Jumeirah Beach Residence (04 423 1987). The boho enclave of The Courtyard (courtyard-uae.com) in Al Quoz has funky furniture and accessories amid its art galleries. Traffic (viatraffic.org) is a gallery, gift shop and studio in Al Barsha that stocks fashion items, interior design pieces and small gifts. The Antique Museum (04 347 9935), in Al Quoz, is full to the brim with everything from souvenirs (not all of them from the UAE), to furniture, pashminas and Omani silver. The prices are less than in tourist hotspots like Souk Madinat Jumeirah and wandering through its passageways and secret rooms is a treat in itself. If you've forgot your iPad charger at home, Sharaf DG (sharafdg.com) is one of the more popular spots to buy electronics. You'll find branches in several of the malls but its largest store is in Times Square Center (800 344 357). For something for the kids – or grownups with a soft spot for sweet treats – head to Candylicious (04 330 8700, candyliciousshop.com). This super-sized sweet shop in The Dubai Mall has enough goodies to keep those with a sweet tooth grinning from ear to ear.

Going Out

Dine, Drink, Dance

Celebrity chefs, world-class nightlife and ethnic eateries; Dubai's dining and entertainment options are endless.

Dubai's gastronomic landscape is huge and constantly growing. Cosmopolitan culinary treats, picturesque bars and cosy shisha joints combine to form the region's most exciting nightlife. The city's varied population and ritzy reputation has produced a demand for exceptional food. Fine-dining aficionados will be impressed with the diversity, quality and abundance of first-rate restaurants, while culinary tourists can dine on authentic Arabic kebabs for lunch and fiery Pakistani curries for dinner.

Thursday and Friday nights are the big ones, with reservations required in the restaurants and international DJs in the clubs. However, during the week you'll find drinks deals across the city and all manner of dining promotions. See Brunch & Other Deals (p.223) for more information. While Dubai doesn't lend itself to pub crawls by foot or evening strolls around

The Yellow Star

The little yellow star highlights venues that merit extra praise. It could be the atmosphere, the food, the cocktails, the music or the crowd, but whatever the reason, any review that you see with the star attached is for somewhere considered a bit special.

restaurant districts, venues tend to be close together, either within a hotel or a mall such as Souk Madinat Jumeirah (p.120), or a short taxi ride away.

Keep in mind that Dubai's licensing laws are unique. For a venue to serve alcohol, it must be attached to a hotel or a sporting facility. This means no supermarket six-packs and no wine at your independent bistro. The legal drinking age is 21, and it's best to avoid getting staggeringly drunk as it may land you behind bars. Most importantly, don't even think about getting behind the wheel of a car after drinking – Dubai maintains a strict zero tolerance stance on drunk driving. Respect the laws and you'll have nothing to worry about – Dubai certainly knows how to throw a party.

Brunch & Other Deals

With so many venues to choose from, Dubai's restaurants and bars face stiff competition in attracting punters. As a result, there are some excellent deals on food and drink almost every day of the week. All-you-can-eat-and-drink deals abound, and some of the city's best restaurants offer time-specific deals that let diners experience exquisite creations at extreme discounts. Tuesday has become the official ladies' night for several of Dubai's drinking institutions, including Healey's (p.310) and Blends (p.305) in the Dubai Marina (p.104), and Margaux (p.276) in Downtown (p.98). Check askexplorer.com for an insider scoop on the latest 'it' venues and the hottest offers when you're in town.

The king of all Dubai deals is the Friday brunch, and a lazy, drawn out, all-you-can-eat-and-drink afternoon is a must for any visitor. Many of the finest five-star hotels, including Al Qasr (p.71), Burj Al Arab (p.69), Park Hyatt Dubai (p.72) and Jumeirah Beach Hotel (p.70) put on lavish spreads every Friday afternoon and they're almost always packed with punters. These all-you-can-eat-and-drink affairs often include unlimited champagne and food from all over the world – sometimes with the option to extend your feast through the evening for an additional fee. Of course, such luxury comes at a price – usually upwards of Dhs.350 for the premium options. If you want to indulge in daytime dining but want to save the dirhams then there are some decent cheaper options, such as Organic Foods & Cafe's Dhs.95 for adults and Dhs.65 for kids option (04 434 0577) and Pergolas (04 321 1111) in the Murooj Rotana, which offers all-you-can-eat-and-drink themed dinner buffets every night of the week.

Double Trouble

Dubai has a number of restaurants that deserve extra credit for their stellar bars. Trader Vic's (p.294) serves some stunning cocktails, while El Malecon (p.263) and Spectrum on One (p.290) are worth a trip for the bar alone. Likewise, several of Dubai's bars, including Caramel (p.308) and Sho Cho's (p.316) serve light bites and bigger plates that are tasty enough to warrant a table reservation.

Vegetarian

There are plenty of delicious local delicacies that will thrill herbivores. Rahib salad, a hot combination of aubergine and tomato, is a great option when eating Lebanese food, or you could go with tasty tabouleh, fattoush and falafel, all served with fluffy fresh bread. See p.10, 227 for more on local cuisine. Middle Eastern food traditions aside, the huge population of south Asians means there are plenty of authentic vegetable curries to be had. Head to Karama (p.130) or Satwa to try a veg thali, which consists of up to 10 small pots of curries, pickles and sauces into which you can dip chapatti, or mix with rice. You'll find plenty of small restaurants in and around Karama; Saravana Bhavan (p.288) is an exceptionally good choice, and the experience will rarely cost you more than Dhs.12.

Karaoke

The draw of the microphone and the lure of crooning embarrassment is alive and well in Dubai, and the city's best karaoke bars are tight and intimate, just as they should be. Harry Ghatto's (04 319 8088) in Emirates Towers is a favourite, Hibiki (04 209 1234) in Galleria Mall has private rooms, and It's Mirchi (04 334 4088) offers a bizarre Indian alternative, complete with plenty of curries and a multi-lingual songbook.

Nightclubs

Massive sound systems, international DJs, incredibly diverse interiors and just enough musical variety to keep things interesting – Dubai's club scene has long been the best in the region, and it keeps getting better. House and popular

R&B dominate Dubai's dancefloors, but some clubs regularly promote theme nights such as Arabic, Indian and cheesy music. Door policies differ from venue to venue. Some of the most exclusive spots, such as Cavalli Club (p.308) and Cirque Du Soir Dubai (04 332 4900), won't let you in unless you're on the guest list, while others like Chi@The Lodge (p.309) merely require a decent pair of shoes.

Street Food

The shawarma is to Dubai what the hot dog is to New York. The popular snack, consisting of rolled pita bread filled with lamb or chicken carved from a rotating spit, can be found throughout the city, and tiny cafeterias serving the delicacy are around every corner. At about Dhs.3 each, they're the perfect end to a big night out or a tasty pre-club snack. Try to avoid shawarma stands that carve from tiny slabs of meat – a huge shawarma spit is a good sign that the cafeteria has a high turnover. Street-side cafeterias also squeeze and press some of the best and least expensive fresh juices in the city.

Shisha

It's common to see people relaxing in the evening with a shisha pipe. Shisha is a popular method of smoking tobacco with a water-filled pipe. It comes in a variety of flavours, including grape and apple. Some of the best places to try shisha in Dubai are Reem Al Bawadi (p.285), and QD's at The Boardwalk (p.258).

Arabian Experience

Al Fanar (p.247) and Bastakiah Nights (p.256) are among the handful of restaurants specialising in local Emirati dishes like al machboos or al harees. In addition, there's plenty of opportunity to experience Arabic food from other parts of the region, especially Lebanon and Syria.

All Aboard

Dinner on the creek is a must. While in town, try the five-star fare of Bateaux Dubai (04 814 5553, bateauxdubai. com). Alternatively, opt for Creek Cruises (04 393 9860, creekcruises. com) for the fun tourist option that comes complete with a belly dancer.

Tabouleh (chopped parsley with bulgar, tomato and herbs), fattoush (salad seasoned with sumac and topped with toasted pita), arayes (grilled flat bread with spiced meat in the middle) and many kinds of grilled, skewered meat can be found in any Arabic restaurant – all of these are great introductions to regional cuisine and no visit should end without sampling the local delicacies at least once. Head to Reem Al Bawadi (p.285) for an authentic first try, chill out at Al Khayma (p.247) over shisha and shish taouk, or book a table at an upscale Arabic eatery such as Levantine (p.272). For the full Arabian experience, try heading out on a desert safari (p.144) where you'll be entertained by a belly dancer, dine on a full array of Arabic delights under the stars and smoke the requisite shisha.

With a popular film festival, massive concerts and a growing theatre scene, Dubai is a regional entertainment hub.

Entertainment

Cinema

Dubai loves going to the movies, and the city's residents flock to the cinemas every weekend. The biggest theatres include a 22 screen Reel Cinema outlet in The Dubai Mall (04 449 1988, reelcinemas.ae) and a 21 screen cinema at Ibn Battuta Mall (Grand Megaplex, grandcinemas.com). Another major player, VOX Cinemas (voxcinemas.com), also has theatres across town, including ones offering 3D content and premium screenings for select films.

Outdoor screenings have become popular of late and movies in the pool has become the latest craze. Wafi (p.212) launched its Movies Under The Stars in 2010, while Dubai Polo & Equestrian Club (04 361 8111, poloclubdubai.com) and The Address Montgomerie (themontgomerie.com) both offer movie screenings outside by the pool during the hotter summer months.

Dubai cinemas tend to mostly show mainstream films, but movie buffs in town during December are in for a treat. The Dubai International Film Festival (p.55) is a definite cinematic highlight that runs for a week in December across various locations in the city and showcases an impressive mix of mainstream, world and local cinema – from short films to full-length features.

Comedy

Comedy nights in Dubai are popular with the expat crowd but events tend to be semi-regular, rather than weekly nights. The Laughter Factory (thelaughterfactory.com) organises monthly performances, with comedians from the UK's Comedy Store coming over to play various venues throughout Dubai, including Zinc (p.319) and The Aviation Club (aviationclub.ae). A lot of comedy is aimed at the expat crowd, so unless you're familiar with the comedian's country, you might not be laughing. Keep an eye on thelaughterfactory.com for details of future shows.

Live Music

Dubai hosts a number of concerts each year, and as the city grows it attracts bigger names. Past acts include Muse, Kanye West, Sting and Robbie Williams. The bigger names usually play at outdoor venues such as the Tennis Stadium, Dubai Autodrome and the amphitheatre at Media City.

In addition to acts at the height of their fame, Dubai also plays host to a string of groups that may be past their prime,

Something Different

Many of the nightclubs in Bur Dubai's three and four-star hotels feature live bands that cater for a certain culture. For African music, head to the Beach Club at the Palm Beach Hotel (04 393 1999) and for a lively Filipino band try Maharlika at the President Hotel (04 334 6565).

but nonetheless provide good entertainment (think Human League, Tony Hadley, Go West, Echo & The Bunnymen and Deacon Blue).

There has been a recent rise in alternative and slightly lesser-known acts coming over for some sun including Groove Armada, 2ManyDJs and Super Furry Animals. Dubai also hosts several music festivals each year focusing on rock, rhythm and world music. For more information on events in Dubai and Abu Dhabi, keep an eye on Explorer's website (askexplorer.com) which has details of events, promotions and upcoming gigs in Dubai and Abu Dhabi.

Theatre

The theatre scene in Dubai remains a little limited but as the city grows, so does its thirst for culture, and with an increase in modern facilities over the past couple of years, theatre lovers finally have something to cheer about. The First Group Theatre (madinattheatre.com) hosts a variety of performances, from serious stage plays to comedies and musical performances. Cirque du Soleil has set up its massive big-top at Ibn Battuta each spring for the past few years and is always a bit hit. The Palladium (palladium-dmc.com), is located in Media City and has hosted acts from Akon to The Wiggles. A local theatre scene is also beginning to thrive – Dubai Community Theatre and Arts Centre (ductac.org) at Mall Of The Emirates provides valuable theatre space for amateur dramatics performances, as well as for smaller-scale shows which have included touring shows from Edinburgh's Fringe festival.

Dubai Community Theatre and Arts Centre

Venue Directory

Cafes & Restaurants

International

Italian

Japanese

Bars, Pubs & Nightclubs

Area Directory

Al Barsha

Restaurants

Bars, Pubs & Clubs

Al Karama

Restaurants

Al Garhoud & Festival City

Restaurants

Bars, Pubs & Clubs

Al Satwa

Restaurants

Al Sufouh & Palm Jumeirah

Restaurants

Bars, Pubs & Clubs

Bahri Bar	Mina A'Salam	p.303
Barasti	Le Meridien Mina Seyahi Beach Resort & Marina	p.304
Barzar	Souk Madinat Jumeirah	p.304
BidiBondi	Clubhouse Al Manhal, Shoreline Apartments	p.305
Jambase	Souk Madinat Jumeirah	p.312
Jetty Lounge	One&Only Royal Mirage	p.313
Oeno Wine Bar	The Westin Dubai Mina Seyahi Beach Resort & Marina	p.314
N'Dulge Nightclub	Atlantis The Palm	p.315
The Agency	Souk Madinat Jumeirah	p.302
The Roof Top & Sports Lounge	One&Only Royal Mirage	p.314
Voda Bar	Jumeirah Zabeel Saray	p.318

Bur Dubai

Restaurants

Basta Art Cafe	The Bastakiya, Al Souk Al Kabeer	p.256
Bastakiah Nights	The Bastakiya	p.256
Troyka	Ascot Hotel	p.296

Deira & Al Rigga

Restaurants

Al Dawaar	Hyatt Regency Dubai	p.247
Ashiana	Sheraton Dubai Creek Hotel & Towers	p.253
Bamboo Lagoon	JW Marriott Hotel Dubai	p.254
Creekside Japanese Restaurant	Sheraton Dubai Creek Hotel & Towers	p.263
Glasshouse Brasserie	Hilton Dubai Creek	p.268
Hofbräuhaus	JW Marriott Hotel Dubai	p.269
JW's Steakhouse	JW Marriott Hotel Dubai	p.271

Downtown Dubai & Sheikh Zayed Road

Restaurants

Dubai Marina, JBR & JLT

Going Out

Area Directory

Siddharta Lounge		
By Buddha Bar	Grosvenor House	p.315
Trader Vic's	Oasis Beach Tower	p.294
Trader Vic's Mai-Tai		
Lounge	Al Fattan Marine Tower II	p.316
The Hub	Sofitel Dubai Jumeirah Beach	p.312
Blends	The Address Dubai Marina	p.306
The Underground	Habtoor Grand Beach	
Pub	Resort & Spa	p.318

Emirates Living
Restaurants
Nineteen	The Address Montgomerie	p.279

Jumeira & Umm Suqeim
Restaurants
Al Khayma	Dubai Marine Beach	
	Resort & Spa	p.247
Al Mahara	Burj Al Arab	p.248
Al Muntaha	Burj Al Arab	p.248
Beachcombers	Jumeirah Beach Hotel	p.257
El Malecon	Dubai Marine Beach	
	Resort & Spa	p.263
Majlis Al Bahar	Burj Al Arab	p.275
Marina	Jumeirah Beach Hotel	p.274
Reem Al Bawadi	Jumeirah Rd, Nr HSBC	p.285
Sahn Eddar	Burj Al Arab	p.288
The Lime Tree	Jumeira Rd,	
Cafe & Kitchen	Nr Jumeira Mosque	p.273
Villa Beach	Jumeirah Beach Hotel	p.296

Bars, Pubs & Clubs
360°	Jumeirah Beach Hotel	p.302
Boudoir	Dubai Marine Beach	
	Resort & Spa	p.306

Dhow & Anchor	Jumeirah Beach Hotel	p.309
Sho Cho	Dubai Marine Beach Resort & Spa	p.316
Skyview Bar	Burj Al Arab	p.316
Uptown Bar	Jumeirah Beach Hotel	p.318

Nad Al Sheba

Restaurants

| The Farm | Al Barari | p.264 |

Oud Metha & Umm Hurair

Restaurants

Asha's	Wafi	p.253
Fakhreldine	Mövenpick Hotel & Apartments Bur Dubai	p.264
Fire & Ice	Raffles Dubai	p.265
iZ	Grand Hyatt Dubai	p.270
Khazana	Al Nasr Leisureland	p.271
Manhattan Grill	Grand Hyatt Dubai	p.275
Peppercrab	Grand Hyatt Dubai	p.283
The Fountain Restaurant	Mövenpick Hotel & Apartments Bur Dubai	p.266

Bars, Pubs & Clubs

| Chi@The Lodge | Al Nasr Leisureland | p.309 |

Port Saeed

Restaurants

Cafe Arabesque	Park Hyatt Dubai	p.260
The Boardwalk	Dubai Creek Golf & Yacht Club	p.258
The Thai Kitchen	Park Hyatt Dubai	p.293
Traiteur	Park Hyatt Dubai	p.296

Bars, Pubs & Clubs

| The Terrace | Park Hyatt Dubai | p.317 |

Restaurants & Cafes

Dubai's culinary landscape includes everything from mountainous buffet spreads to low-key streetside snacks.

There isn't much you can't find in Dubai when it comes to food; whether it's a quick-fix burger, super fresh fish and chips or sizzling curries, the variety is extraordinary. Dining in one of Dubai's five-star hotel resorts is a must, if only to witness the tremendous variety and quality. Bookings are not always necessary, but it is best to check as hotel guests often get first dibs on the tables and popular restaurants do fill up quickly.

Alternatively, bypass Michelin-starred options and still get fare that is both tasty and easy on the wallet. Visitors should experience some of Dubai's more modest, but certainly vibrant and atmospheric, independent Indian restaurants such as Saravana Bhavan (p.288) and popular Pakistani restaurant Ravi's (p.284). There are also several Arabic restaurants (p.232) that are worth a try. Al Mallah (p.248) on 2nd Of December Road in Satwa is a popular spot for pavement dining, shawarmas and juices at very reasonable prices.

When it comes to breakfast and lunch, you can grab a bite at the delightful cafes loved by Dubai's expats such as MORE Cafe (04 283 0224, morecafe.biz), Shakespeare & Co. (04 331 1757), Lime Tree Cafe (p.273) and Epicure (04 323 888). For real cafe culture Dubai-style, stroll along The Walk, Jumeirah Beach Residence, which offers up a wide selection of restaurants and cafes, and plenty of opportunity to people-watch along its bustling beachfront promenade.

Al Dawaar

International

Hyatt Regency Dubai, Corniche, Deira 04 317 2222

Revolving restaurant may evoke images or pure kitsch, but Al Dawaar is a surprisingly sophisticated buffet haunt and the slow revolution (it takes one hour and 45 minutes to do a complete turn) gives you an interesting window on this side of town.

Map 4 D1 **Metro** Palm Deira

Al Fanar Restaurant & Cafe

Emirati

Dubai Festival Centre, Dubai Festival City 04 232 9966

Ask to be seated in one of the majlis (tent) spots here and get prepared to while away the hours sipping tea and relaxing. The indoor section reveals a bustling scene from the old town where you can take your pick and enjoy lunch or dinner at the Pearl Merchants House, Bait Al Tawash (courtyard) or Souq. Each offers a fabulous setting for your meal, and the food itself is a superb introduction to traditional Emirati food (p.10).

Map 1 J4 **Metro** Emirates

Al Khayma

Arabic/Lebanese

Dubai Marine Beach Resort & Spa, Jumeira 1 04 346 1111

Turn up at this popular Lebanese haunt for a small bite of Beirut – the atmosphere is lively, and the tempting sofas perfect for whiling away the hours over shisha, drinks and tasty Levantine bites: the veggie platter with dips is the way to go for starters before tucking into piping-hot barbecue grub and shish kebabs. Wash it all down with fresh juices or opt for Lebanese wine. **Map** 1 H2 **Metro** Al Jafiliya

Al Mahara

Seafood

Burj Al Arab, Umm Suqeim 3
04 301 7600

Your visit to Al Mahara starts with a simulated submarine ride that takes you 'under the sea' to dine among the fish. 'Disembark' and you'll see the restaurant is curled around a huge aquarium. This is fine dining at its finest, with prices to match. Gentlemen are required to wear a jacket for dinner.

Map 3 E1 **Metro** Mall Of The Emirates

Al Mallah

Arabic/Lebanese

2nd Of December Rd, Al Hudaiba
04 398 4723

Al Mallah offers great pavement dining with an excellent view of the world and his brothers cruising by in their Ferraris. The shawarmas and fruit juices are excellent, the cheese and zatar manoushi exceedingly tasty, and it has possibly the biggest and best falafel in Dubai. The incongruous 'Diana' and 'Charles' shakes are recommended.

Map 1 H2 **Metro** Al Jafiliya

Al Muntaha

Mediterranean

Burj Al Arab, Umm Suqeim 3
04 301 7600

If you weren't at the top of the Burj Al Arab, with an unrivalled view of Dubai's coastline, you would be forgiven for thinking this restaurant's decor is a bit tacky considering the price tag. The menu is less surprising than the decor, with the usual suspects in a European fine-dining line-up. The food is certainly good, despite an atmosphere akin to a private members' club.

Map 3 E1 **Metro** Mall Of The Emirates

Al Mahara

Al Nafoorah

Arabic/Lebanese

Boulevard At Jumeirah Emirates
Towers, Trade Centre 2   04 319 8088

The menu at this highly rated Lebanese restaurant is extensive, with pages and pages of mezze and mains to tantalise. It's best to come in a group and share the wide selection. After dinner, you can take a stroll round The Boulevard, or sit out and enjoy shisha in front of the looming Emirates Towers.

Map 2 D2 **Metro** Emirates Towers

Al Samadi Cafe & Sweet Shop
Arabic/Lebanese

Financial Centre Rd, Downtown Dubai   04 432 9520

A wonderful old-school sweet shop with a classy cafe, Al Samadi is evocative of old Paris or Beirut and the savoury menu follows the Franco-Lebanese theme; the Caesar salad comes with shish taouk, the rocket salad with grilled halloumi. Whatever time of day you visit, you will likely find it hard to leave without a beautifully packaged parcel of baklava or knaffeh. **Map** 2 B3 **Metro** Burj Khalifa/Dubai Mall

Amwaj
Seafood

Shangri-La Hotel, Trade Centre 1   04 405 2703

The minimal decor here cleverly depicts a marine theme yet remains refined. An immaculate sushi bar greets you, and the open kitchen allows you to watch tantalising dishes being prepared. The menu offers endless fish and seafood creations, and the vegetarian and meat choices are equally impressive, especially the foie gras. **Map** 2 C1 **Metro** Financial Centre

AOC
French

Sofitel Dubai, Jumeirah Beach, Dubai Marina   04 448 4848

The staff are friendly and the venue, especially the terrace, make AOC a good dining option in JBR – as long as you arrive with the awareness that the a la carte menu features largely European main courses rather than anything authentically French. However, the quality of food is excellent and the wine list and desserts do their best to return a touch of Gallic oooh la la to proceedings.

Map 3 A1 **Metro** Jumeirah Lakes Towers

Après

International

Mall Of The Emirates, Al Barsha 1   04 341 2575

This cosy alpine ski lodge has a comfortable bar area and an unrivalled view of the Ski Dubai slope. The varied menu offers wholesome fare including steaks, fondue and excellent pizzas. During the day, it's great for families but, at night, the laidback vibe and cocktail list encourage chilled dining and socialising. **Map** 3 E2 **Metro** Mall Of The Emirates

Aquara

International

Dubai Marina Yacht Club, Dubai Marina   04 362 7900

Chic but understated, Aquara allows the view of million-dirham yachts to speak for itself. The menu features options that range from sophisticated burgers to chic, lighter fare with a definite emphasis on seafood, most of which comes with an Asian twist. Friday brunch is excellent value at Dhs.220, or Dhs.290 with house drinks; also available in the evening. The centrepiece is the seafood bar with lobsters, oysters, prawns, crabs, clams, sushi and sashimi.

Map 3 A1 **Metro** Jumeirah Lakes Towers

Arabesque Cafe

Arabic/Lebanese

Arjaan By Rotana Dubai Media City, Al Sufouh 1   04 436 0145

Decorated in the style of a traditional Arabian palace – and enhanced by ornate lighting, plush, purple soft furnishings, traditional ornaments and decorative touches – this pleasant restaurant specialises in Middle Eastern fare. It's mainly a buffet format, including a breakfast and lunch buffet, as well as the Friday brunch. **Map** 3 B1 **Metro** Nakheel

Armani/Amal

Indian

Armani Hotel Dubai, Downtown Dubai   04 888 3888

The Armani Hotel's Indian restaurant was always going to be a special place, and it has been a huge success, winning awards and admirers from the day it opened. With its open kitchen and vaulted framework, the dining room evokes a hip nightspot in a converted Indian marketplace. Orange and blue lightshades brighten the Armani colour palette and the food is vibrant high-end Indian cuisine.

Map 2 B2 **Metro** Burj Khalifa/Dubai Mall

Armani/Peck

Italian

Armani Hotel Dubai, Downtown Dubai   04 888 3888

In keeping with the Armani style of less-is-more, this black and white restaurant's decor is like the food on offer: simple and tasty, beautifully presented Italian fare. Diners can choose to go a la carte or opt for the sharing concept, a set menu that takes you on a culinary journey through the boot country. In addition to Italian treats, there's also a selection of Arabic meats and sweets.

Map 2 B2 **Metro** Burj Khalifa/Dubai Mall

Asado

Argentinean

The Palace Downtown Dubai   04 888 3444

A combination of moody lighting, passionate music, a killer location and a meat lovers' dream menu cement Asado's position as one of Dubai's top steakhouses. Excellent quality cuts cooked to any carnivore's delight are exquisite and the enormous wine selection is bound to have something to suit most tastes as well. Add to this the terrace views of Burj Khalifa and you've got a formula that makes this Argentinean restaurant something very special.

Map 2 B3 **Metro** Burj Khalifa/Dubai Mall

Asha's

Indian

Wafi, Umm Hurair 2   04 324 4100

Owned by Indian superstar Asha Bhosle, this Dubai favourite offers a memorable dining experience. Decked out in summer colours of reds, yellows, and oranges, the space features beaded curtains, low-level lighting, and intimate booths as well as an inviting terrace. The menu features a few Indian favourites plus a selection of Asha's very own signature dishes picked up on her travels.

Map 4 B5 **Metro** Healthcare City

Ashiana

Indian

Sheraton Dubai Creek Hotel & Towers, Al Rigga   04 207 1733

With empire-inspired decor and a traditional band playing authentic tunes every night, Ashiana celebrates India's colonial era. Cosy booths around the walls are the seats of choice, unless you're in a large group. The staff deserve a special mention for their swift and friendly service.

Map 4 D3 **Metro** Union

At.mosphere

International

Burj Khalifa, Downtown Dubai   04 888 3444

The world's highest restaurant was always going to be big on the wow factor, but the kitchen manages to deliver on the

lofty ambition with opulent menus of premium ingredients and exquisite presentation. Open for lunch and dinner, this really is the ultimate in high-end dining destinations – and has to be the finest sundowner spot anywhere.
Map 2 B2 **Metro** Burj Khalifa/Dubai Mall

AZ.U.R   Mediterranean
Dubai Marriott Harbour Hotel
  & Suites, Dubai Marina   04 319 4794

AZ.U.R offers a range of simple but tasty meat, fish and seafood dishes, as well as fresher-than-fresh vegetables, all served in a non-fussy style that lets the ingredients do the talking. The menu features cuisine of France, Morocco, Spain and Italy – think hearty onion soup, mezze, deep-fried calamari and Bolognaise. The sizeable portions are unlikely to leave you hungry and you can digest it all while enjoying a shisha on the large terrace, which boasts lovely views to boot.
Map 3 B1 **Metro** Dubai Marina

Bamboo Lagoon   Far Eastern
JW Marriott Hotel Dubai, Al Muraqqabat   04 607 7977

With a little bridge and a big crocodile, you won't forget this restaurant's decor in a hurry. The food is memorable too: there's sushi, tempura, teriyaki, curries, stir-fries, grills, seafood, rice and noodle dishes. All are equally tempting and so wonderfully presented that you'll wish you hadn't eaten that big lunch. At 21:00 a band takes to the stage and grass-skirted singers serenade diners with low-key renditions of tropical tunes. **Map** 4 E4 **Metro** Abu Baker Al Siddique

Bastakiah Nights

Basta Art Cafe

Cafe

Bastakiya, Al Souk Al Kabeer

04 353 5071

This courtyard cafe and gallery offers quiet sanctuary amid busy and atmospheric Bastakiya. Sit on majlis-style cushions or under a canopy while choosing from the healthy dishes and fresh juices; the Arabic breakfast is a good option if you're in this area in the morning.

Map 4 C2 **Metro** Al Fahidi

Bastakiah Nights

Arabic/Lebanese

Bastakiya, Al Souk Al Kabeer

04 353 7772

As you enter through heavy wooden doors you are reminded that, despite the glitzy malls and luxurious hotels, Dubai is still very much Arabia. The regional fare on offer is faultless and you can choose between fixed menus and a la carte offerings such as lamb stew and stuffed vine leaves. There's no alcohol licence.

Map 4 C2 **Metro** Al Fahidi

Beach Bar & Grill

Seafood

The Palace At One&Only Royal Mirage,
 Al Sufouh 1

04 399 9999

This superb restaurant is definitely one to pull out when you want a truly romantic evening. Seafood lovers must make a trip to this opulent, intimate beach bar. Terrace tables are candle-lit, and the fresh fish is cooked simply but with style. Seafood platters to share, and surf and turf options, are available for people who simply can't pick just one dish.

Map 3 B1 **Metro** Nakheel

Beachcombers

Far Eastern

Jumeirah Beach Hotel, Umm Suqeim 3   04 406 8999

This breezy shack has an idyllic location right on the beach with fantastic views of the Burj Al Arab. Expect excellent Far Eastern buffets with live cooking stations for stir-fries and noodles. The Peking duck, curry hotpots and satay are highly recommended.

Map 3 A1 **Metro** Mall Of The Emirates

BiCE Mare

Italian

Souk Al Bahar, Downtown Dubai   04 423 0982

An idyllic location, delicious dishes in all shapes, sizes, both simple and complex, and an intimate yet relaxed atmosphere all combine to make this Mediterranean restaurant a serious contender in Souk Al Bahar. Dine inside and be entertained by the sultry jazz hands of the resident pianist or take in the splendid Dubai Fountain show from the terrace. A sister to BiCE, the Mare signifies a seafood dominated menu that will bring fish lovers back time and time again.

Map 2 B3 **Metro** Burj Khalifa/Dubai Mall

Blue Elephant

Thai

Al Bustan Rotana, Al Garhoud   04 282 0000

If a trip to Thailand is out of the question, walking into Blue Elephant comes a close second. While sitting at bamboo tables, gazing into a lagoon and surrounded by tropical greenery, the smell of orchids is evocative of exotic Far Eastern climes and the menu showcases an array of Thai classics, spiced to your liking. **Map** 4 E6 **Metro** GGICO

Blue Flame
Seafood

Jumeirah Creekside Hotel, Al Garhoud   04 230 8580

The flagship restaurant of Jumeirah Creekside specialises in creative seafood and steak dishes. Head here for a fine-dining experience with refreshingly innovative culinary touches, evident in combinations such as savoury muffins with shiitake mushrooms and broccoli, served with lobster butter.

Map 4 D6 **Metro** GGICO

The Boardwalk
International

Dubai Creek Golf & Yacht Club, Port Saeed   04 295 6000

Positioned on wooden stilts over the creek, The Boardwalk boasts a view that is virtually unmatched in Dubai – and the menu can't be faulted either. Varied enough to suit all tastes, it features a range of international dishes and the drinks list is equally extensive: there's a huge selection of cocktails and mocktails. Just next door sits QD's, which shares the same incredible views but concentrates more on drinks and shisha.

Map 4 C6 **Metro** Deira City Centre

BoHouse Cafe
Cafe

The Walk, Jumeirah Beach Residence   04 429 8655

There's no shortage of casual eateries on the JBR Walk, but BoHouse's enviable location between the street and shore sets the artsy cafe-cum-restaurant apart from most: whether you turn up for breakfast or shisha on the breezy terrace or opt for lunch by the floor-to-ceiling windows indoors, the beach view is among the best along this busy stretch.

Map 3 A1 **Metro** Dubai Marina

Clockwise from top left: Blue Elephant, The Cellar, The Boardwalk

Bussola

Italian

The Westin Dubai Mina Seyahi Beach Resort
& Marina, Al Sufouh 1   04 399 4141

Famed for its pizzas, Bussola is a longstanding favourite
among the locals. A Sicilian influence on the menu means
the choices are slightly more adventurous than your standard
Italian fare, and you should definitely save room for dessert
as well. The open-air first-floor veranda serves cocktails to a
backdrop of sparkling sea views and chill-out tunes.
Map 3 B1 **Metro** Nakheel

The Butcher Shop & Grill

Steakhouse

Mall Of The Emirates, Al Barsha 1   04 347 1167

Shoppers with a taste for hearty meat dishes need not look
further than this Kempinski joint with easy access from Mall
Of The Emirates: pick your fillet, rump, T-bone or prime rib
and watch in awe as the giant man-size portions are served
up. This is also a good option should you get hungry during
an afternoon spent in the cool climes of Ski Dubai (p.156).
Map 3 E2 **Metro** Mall Of The Emirates

Cafe Arabesque

Arabic/Lebanese

Park Hyatt Dubai, Port Saeed   04 317 2222

Whether you choose buffet or a la carte, linger over a cold
mezze spread, succulent wood-fired kebabs and other,
fantastic Lebanese, Syrian and Jordanian dishes as you take
in marvellous views of the creek. With romantic, soft lighting,
the perfect evening awaits.
Map 4 C5 **Metro** GGICO

Can Can Brasserie
French

The Ritz-Carlton, Dubai International
Financial Centre, Trade Centre 2 04 372 2222

This casual-chic venue serves brasserie fare in a Parisian-style setting just steps away from the hustle and bustle of DIFC. Classics from escargots to steak frites grace the menu and you can choose to sit indoors or out in the courtyard. The Express Lunch offers excellent value; for Dhs.75, you get to sample the delicious starter buffet before being served the main course of your choice.

Map 2 D2 **Metro** Emirates Towers

The Cellar
International

The Aviation Club, Al Garhoud 04 282 9333

Diners enjoy their own space in a well-lit room of soaring arches and unexpected stained glass. The outside terrace is also pleasantly relaxed. The a la carte Saturday brunch is recommended. The Cellar's international menu has some favourites and some innovations and the wine list, with special bargains on Saturday and Sunday evenings, shows a surprisingly unusual range.

Map 4 D6 **Metro** GGICO

Center Cut
Steakhouse

The Ritz-Carlton, Dubai International
Financial Centre, Trade Centre 2 04 372 2323

Located close to DIFC, this is a good option for carnivores in the heart of Dubai's financial district. The restaurant's speciality is evident from the start: the first page of the menu

is adorned with a diagram of a cow and the cuts of meat, and while the appetisers include non-carnivorous items such as Atlantic salmon and foie gras, your main meal is really all about the steaks here. Choose from Australian or American cuts with a selection of sauces and sides to accompany your chosen one.
Map 2 D2 **Metro** Financial Centre

The China Club
Chinese

Radisson Blu Hotel, Dubai Deira Creek, Al Rigga   04 222 7171

A chic space, with subtle touches of authenticity, serving familiar favourites from all over China. The Peking duck, carved at the table, is a great choice from the a la carte menu, while the daily lunchtime buffet, Yum Cha, offers excellent value: for Dhs.99, you get to sample a feast of dim sum, noodles and other Chinese specialities, along with tea and soft drinks. **Map** 4 D2 **Metro** Union

Counter Culture
Cafe

Dubai Marriott Harbour Hotel & Suites   04 319 4000

Deli delights and easy-going vibes lie within this little gem of a cafe in this end of Dubai Marina. The cosy joint features relaxing leather chairs, wooden furniture and a contemporary colour scheme. The bread is guaranteed to be freshly-baked – so much so that you can actually watch it being prepared. In addition, daily hot and cold specials, big salads, chunky sandwiches and home-made ice cream is what's on offer here. The venue is licensed and open from 06:00 to 17:00.
Map 3 B1 **Metro** Dubai Marina

Creekside Restaurant

Japanese

Sheraton Dubai Creek Hotel & Towers, Al Rigga   04 207 1750

One of the recommended Japanese restaurants in the city, Creekside now runs 'theme nights' every night of the week. In other words, it has become an all-you-can-eat paradise for fans of food from the land of the rising sun. The restaurant's interior reflects Japanese aesthetics and style, and the spacious grounds make a great setting for larger groups.

Map 4 D3 **Metro** Union

Eauzone

Far Eastern

Arabian Court At One&Only Royal Mirage,
Al Sufouh 1   04 399 9999

One of the most romantic restaurants in Dubai, Eauzone has poolside tables, low lighting and sublime flavours. The Asian inspired options include sushi, scallops, risotto and Thai prawns but, with curve balls such as foie gras thrown in, you'll find seducing surprises too.

Map 3 C1 **Metro** Nakheel

El Malecon

Cuban

Dubai Marine Beach Resort & Spa, Jumeira 1   04 346 1111

El Malecon's high turquoise walls, big windows that overlook a glowing lagoon and low lighting create a sultry Cuban atmosphere that builds up slowly during the course of the evening, helped along by the live music and Salsa dancers. The menu isn't massive (the signature paella is the best choice), but the lively vibe helps make it up.

Map 1 H2 **Metro** World Trade Centre

The Exchange Grill

Steakhouse

Fairmont Dubai, Trade Centre 1 · 04 311 8316

The Exchange Grill is the epitome of excess with outsized leather armchairs, modern art installations and a floor-to-ceiling chandelier. The menu strikes balances classicism and innovation, and both lunch and dinner menus offer the best quality beef.

Map 2 E1 **Metro** World Trade Centre

Fakhreldine

Arabic/Lebanese

Mövenpick Hotel & Apartments
Bur Dubai, Oud Metha · 04 336 6000

From your first dip into the creamy hummus to the last crumb of Arabic sweets, the quality is apparent and the bill isn't too painful to stomach either. Choose from rarer Arabic dishes and old favourites as you watch the gyrating belly dancer strut her stuff to exotic tunes.

Map 4 B5 **Metro** Oud Metha

The Farm

International

Al Barari, Nad Al Sheba · 04 392 5660

Located within the fancy residential district of Al Barari, this new restaurant lies a good 20-30 minute drive outside the city. However, the trek is worth it if you'd like to sample locally-produced food in a stylish setting that's tranquil enough to make it feel like a real escape from the bright lights of Dubai. With plenty of healthy meals on the menu, this is also a good option for anyone watching their waistline.

Map 1 F5

Fakhreldine

Fire & Ice

Raffles Dubai, Umm Hurair 2

International
04 324 8888

Once a molecular gastronomy experiment, Fire & Ice has reinvented itself and transformed into an upscale steakhouse, complete with a signature sauce and top-notch cuts. The service is what you'd expect from a Raffles restaurant, the steaks well prepared and you get to wash it all down with a sip of something from the massive wine list.

Map 4 B5 **Metro** Healthcare City

Fish Market

Seafood

Radisson Blu Hotel, Dubai Deira Creek, Al Rigga   04 222 7171

This is the destination of choice for seafood aficionados. Accompanied by a member of staff clad in plastic gloves and clutching a wicker shopping basket, you can select fresh fish, then request the style of cooking. While you wait for your tailor-made dinner to arrive, you can snack on a bowl of french fries and soak up the creekside view.

Map 4 D2 **Metro** Union

Flavours On Two

International

Towers Rotana, Trade Centre 1   04 312 2202

This stylish, busy 'dinner brunch' venue focuses on a different global cuisine each night, including British and Italian. The wide range of dishes includes cold starters, hot grills and delicious desserts. Free-flowing alcohol is included in the reasonable cover charge, or you can upgrade to champagne by forking out a few extra dirhams.

Map 2 C1 **Metro** Financial Centre

Fountain Restaurant

International

Mövenpick Hotel & Apartments
 Bur Dubai, Oud Metha   04 336 6000

The Movenpick Bur Dubai may be an established hotel, but their new Full Monty Brunch is a welcome addition: the weekend brunch is a truly British feast, with typical pub grub expertly delivered – indeed, it is the sheer size of their signature fry-up that draws in the crowd.

Map 4 B5 **Metro** Oud Metha

Fish Market

Gaucho
Steakhouse

Dubai International Financial Centre,
04 422 7898
Trade Centre 2

This Argentinian-inspired steakhouse caters for carnivores with a soft-spot for trendy settings and Latin culinary touches. The ultra-modern decor comes complete with rustic cowhide upholstery, while items such as chimichurri add an exotic twist on the menu. Gaucho is set on two floors; the restaurant itself is downstairs, while the upstairs lounge offers a bar menu and drinks. **Map** 2 D2 **Metro** Emirates Towers

Giannino
Italian

Meydan Beach, Dubai Marina
04 433 3777

An offshoot of a Milanese dining institution by the same name, Giannino brings a slice of continental culinary tradition to JBR. Northern Italian classics grace the menu and while the beach club setting may not be as authentic as the original venue, this is certainly among your top choices when it comes to Italian food in this part of town.
Map 3 1A **Metro** Jumeirah Lakes Towers

Glasshouse Brasserie
International

Hilton Dubai Creek, Al Rigga
04 227 1111

Sample a taste of the Mediterranean at this chic brasserie with glass walls, dark woods, tasteful colours and Mondrian-style paintings. The menu provides contemporary dishes with a touch of flair. It's a good spot for a business lunch or a lively group dinner. A Friday brunch is available with free-flowing drink options, including champagne. **Map** 4 D3 **Metro** Al Rigga

Hakkasan
Chinese
Jumeirah Emirates Towers, Trade Centre 2   04 384 8484

What works in London or New York doesn't always translate to Dubai, but Hakkasan gets it right. The sleek decor fuses familiar Hakkasan design cues with decidedly Dubai-esque touches such as the spectacular terrace, while the menu remains faithful to the tried-and-tested Hakkasan formula: whether you opt for dim sum, crispy duck salad or the excellent stewed wagyu beef, you're unlikely to be disappointed. The impeccable experience may not come cheap, but this is as good as high-end dining gets in Dubai.

Map 2 D2 **Metro** Emirates Towers

Hofbräuhaus
German
JW Marriott Hotel Dubai, Al Muraqqabat   04 607 7977

From the sauerkraut to the white sausage with sweet mustard, everything here is authentically Bavarian. Add in the beer hall decor, traditional garb for the staff and accordion music and you have a recipe for a fun night out. Several German beers are on tap, along with a full selection of wines.

Map 4 E4 **Metro** Abu Baker Al Siddique

Imperium
French
Jumeirah Zabeel Saray, Palm Jumeirah   04 453 0444

This French restaurant is headed by Jean Hurstel, a talented chef whose skills in Parisian cuisine transcend into the main courses, all of which are served in a petite stainless steel pan, making it easy to pass the dishes around for guests to share.

Map 1 C2 **Metro** Nakheel

The Ivy
International

Boulevard At Jumeirah Emirates Towers,
Trade Centre 2
04 319 8767

The Ivy's modern, brasserie-style menu is loyal to the original London venue: British treats from fish and chips to porkbelly and black pudding are executed with finesse, as are the lighter options that feature many Thai-inspired fusion creations. With tinted glass and green leather, the decor is equally evocative of the original West End setting.

Map 2 D2 **Metro** Emirates Towers

iZ
Indian

Grand Hyatt Dubai, Umm Hurair 2
04 317 2222

iZ's dark, contemporary interior is a beautifully designed space, complete with hardwood screens, sculptures and private rooms. The dishes are presented tapas style – ideal for sampling several flavours. Expect gourmet Indian cuisine that respects tradition. **Map** 4 B6 **Metro** Healthcare City

Jamie's Italian
Italian

Festival Centre, Festival City
04 232 9969

British celebrity chef, caped crusader for organic food and saviour of children's school dinners, Jamie Oliver has decided not to chase after the big bucks but go for the mid-range family market at his namesake Dubai haunt. The menu features antipasti and a selection of tasty pastas which come chunky and fresh, while the mains cover the usual suspects – a burger, steak and Jamie's signature baked fish parcel.

Map 1 J4 **Metro** Emirates

JW's Steakhouse
Steakhouse

JW Marriott Hotel Dubai, Al Muraqqabat
04 607 7977

Set in an intimate, secluded part of the hotel, JW's Steakhouse makes its intentions clear the moment you walk through the door when chefs can be seen cleaving huge chunks of meat in the open kitchen. Once you are shown to your stately leather armchair, a huge menu offering an impressive range of steak and seafood awaits.

Map 4 E4 **Metro** Abu Baker Al Siddique

Karat
Afternoon Tea

The Address Dubai Mall, Downtown Dubai
04 438 8888

Afternoon tea doesn't come much more professional than this. You get to choose from a vast selection of 26 teas, and the sides are served in four courses starting with scones, madeleines, jams and Devonshire cream; then a selection of bite size finger sandwiches arrive, followed by an array of miniature cakes, pastries and Arabic sweets.

Map 2 C2 **Metro** Burj Khalifa/Dubai Mall

Khazana
Indian

Al Nasr Leisureland, Oud Metha
04 336 0061

Indian celebrity chef Sanjeev Kapoor's spacious, popular eatery specialises in cuisine from northern India. All dishes are well-prepared and served in big portions, but the prawn curry and chicken tikka are the most popular. Other delicacies include grilled tandoori seafood, a variety of rice dishes and some hearty gravy options.

Map 4 B4 **Metro** Oud Metha

Kosebasi
Turkish

The Walk, Jumeirah Beach Residence
04 439 3788

Kosebasi's friendly staff take you on a culinary tour of Anatolia right in the heart of JBR Walk. The mezze, breads and kebabs all have a hint of familiarity, but are surprisingly different to standard Arabic fare, offering a welcome choice. Outside, the pavement terrace is bustling.

Map 3 A1 **Metro** Dubai Marina

La Petite Maison
French

Dubai International Financial Centre (DIFC),
Trade Centre 2
04 439 0505

This classy, unfussy restaurant is like a clean, white canvas on which the dining experience can paint itself. The French staff, dressed in bow ties and stripy aprons flit between tables as the chefs beaver away in the open kitchen. The menu features typically Gallic dishes without the cliches – this is the real deal – simple and delicious food with uncomplicated flavours, in which the high quality fresh produce speaks volumes.

Map 2 C2 **Metro** Financial Centre

Levantine
Arabic/Lebanese

Atlantis The Palm, Palm Jumeirah
04 426 2626

This is one of Dubai's ultimate upscale Lebanese dining venues. Popular set menus provide a delicious spread of mezze, mains and desserts, and an extensive a la carte menu allows the more adventurous to try new dishes. The wine list includes some Lebanese delights, while belly dancing and shisha complete the experience. **Map** 1 C1 **Metro** Nakheel

The Lobby Lounge

The Lime Tree Cafe & Kitchen

Cafe

Nr Jumeira Mosque, Jumeira Rd, Jumeira   04 349 8498

Set in a converted villa on Jumeira Road, this impressive cafe has become a Dubai institution and a firm favourite among the local expat ladies (also known as 'Jumeira Janes'). The understated interior features trendy plastic chairs, dark wood tables and lime-green washed walls. With a definite nod towards Mediterranean cuisine, there's plenty of paninis filled with wholesome ingredients, as well as delicious couscous salads and satay kebabs – and quite possibly the best carrot cake in the city. The coffee is also worth a special mention.

Map 1 H2 **Metro** Al Jafiliya

Lobby Lounge
The Ritz-Carlton Dubai, Dubai Marina

Afternoon Tea
04 399 4000

Tea at the Ritz is an exquisite experience. Delicate finger sandwiches and dainty pastries, succulent scones with clotted cream and a selection of jams, a fabulously colonial selection of teas and the fine china are all deliciously regal. It feels exclusive, but all are welcome.
Map 3 A1 **Metro** Dubai Marina

Long Yin
Le Meridien Dubai, Al Garhoud

Chinese
04 702 2325

This perennial Chinese favourite has recently gone through a revamp and, in addition to a sleek new decor, it now boasts one of the best dim sum selections in Dubai. The rest of the menu features skillfully prepared Cantonese and Schezwan favourites and the quality of the food remains top-notch.
Map 4 E6 **Metro** GGICO

Luciano's
Habtoor Grand Beach Resort & Spa,
Dubai Marina

Italian

04 399 5000

Good quality dishes from across Italy are served at this pleasant poolside restaurant. The portions are generous; the starters, ranging from calamari fritti to mozzarella and tomato, are particularly noteworthy in this regard. The real star of the show, however, is the selection of thin-crust pizzas, which are among the best in town. When the weather is conducive, ask for a table outside underneath the fairy-light bedecked palm trees. **Map** 3 B1 **Metro** Dubai Marina

M's Beef Bistro

Steakhouse

Le Meridien Dubai, Al Garhoud

04 702 2455

M's Beef Bistro is unpretentious with an opulent feel, offering excellent service and cuisine in the mid-price range. Ideal for a smart lunch or dinner, the wine list is comprehensive and the menu offers excellent steaks and French dishes; look out for le classiques including French onion soup and burgundy snails.

Map 4 E6 **Metro** GGICO

Majlis Al Bahar

Mediterranean

Burj Al Arab, Umm Suqeim 3

04 301 7600

Part of the Burj Al Arab, Majlis Al Bahar offers front row seats to the iconic hotel's nightly light show. The meaty Mediterranean cuisine isn't exceptional but the mini barbecues are a novel attraction, and the salads are well executed. Come prepared to spend some dirhams – this one certainly isn't for the cost conscious.

Map 3 E1 **Metro** Mall Of The Emirates

Manhattan Grill

Steakhouse

Grand Hyatt Dubai, Umm Hurair 2

04 317 2222

Compared to the indoor rainforest of the hotel's lobby, Manhattan Grill is the ultimate in low-key chic. Soft lighting, plush seating, smooth music and an excellent selection of succulent steaks make this a good choice for fine-dining in a very pleasant setting.

Map 4 B6 **Metro** Healthcare City

Margaux

French

Souk Al Bahar, Downtown Dubai

04 439 7555

Although many factors jostle for your attention here, including the view of the Burj Khalifa, the impressive fountains (p.100) and the extensive wine list, the experience is surprisingly balanced and perfect for a sophisticated night out. French and Italian cuisines mingle successfully on the menu to provide a bit of sustenance in-between the drinks and soaking up the sights.

Map 2 B3 **Metro** Burj Khalifa/Dubai Mall

The Market Place

International

JW Marriott Hotel Dubai, Al Muraqqabat

04 607 7977

Friendly and welcoming, The Market Place is another of Dubai's top all-you-can-eat restaurants. No sooner have you sat down than the waiter brings what will undoubtedly be the first beverage of many, but it's the food that distinguishes this buffet restaurant which has live cooking stations and a most impressive buffet of starters and desserts.

Map 4 E4 **Metro** Abu Baker Al Siddique

Marrakech

Moroccan

Shangri-La Hotel, Trade Centre 1

04 405 2703

Smooth arches and lamps add to an overwhelming sense of tranquillity, while a duo belts out traditional tunes on Marrakech's small stage. Starters such as wedding pie with pigeon, crushed almonds and icing sugar are served on blue ceramic. Don't miss the lamb tagine with fluffy, fragrant rice.

Map 2 C1 **Metro** Financial Centre

Pai Thai

The Meat Co

Steakhouse

Souk Al Bahar, Downtown Dubai — 04 420 0737

This popular South African chain is more than just a string of steakhouses. The well-planned decor matches the thoughtful menu. Start with a mezze appetiser platter, then move on to a healthy lamb skewer with peppers, or an enormous steak with your choice of carbs. There is another restaurant at Souk Madinat Jumeirah (04 368 6040); the alfresco setting by the canals makes this branch a great choice for an evening out, or an earlier family meal, followed up by a stroll around the souk's waterside pathways.

Map 2 B3 **Metro** Burj Khalifa/Dubai Mall

Méridien Village Terrace

International

Le Meridien Dubai, Al Garhoud — 04 702 2455

Only open in winter and beautifully lit at night, this large space manages to feel intimate for couples but is also perfect for larger groups. Each night there is a different culinary theme: Caribbean, Mexican, BBQ or Arabic. Numerous live-cooking stations keep the food wonderfully fresh, while the drinks are replenished with alarming regularity.

Map 4 E6 **Metro** GGICO

Nasimi Beach

International

Atlantis The Palm, Palm Jumeirah — 04 426 2626

Nasimi's formula is simple: it fuses party vibes with a small menu of seafood and meat coupled with one of the best alfresco settings in the city. The large terrace offers views of either the pool or the Palm and as you soak up the vistas, it's hard to imagine a better spot for a day of lounging. The beachside beanbags area turns into a popular place to see and be seen on weekend evenings.

Map 1 C1 **Metro** Nakheel

Nina
Indian

Arabian Court At One&Only Royal Mirage,
Al Sufouh 1 04 399 9999

Flickering candles and heavy velvet curtains set the scene at the One&Only's stylish Indo-European option, Nina. If hearty curries and all-empowering fieriness is what you're after, you're better off looking elsewhere – the food at Nina brings you on an altogether more refined culinary journey to India. Think subtle spiciness and refreshingly novel takes on Indian classics. Amazing cocktails and Indian wine complete the dining experience.

Map 3 C1 **Metro** Nakheel

Nineteen
European

The Address Montgomerie Dubai,
Emirates Living 04 888 3444

The Montgomerie's flagship restaurant serves up rotisserie-style food in chic surroundings and the show kitchen is loud and proud. With views over the hotel's lush grounds, Nineteen is a popular spot among local expats looking to indulge in the restaurant's Friday brunch. For an even more relaxed – but no less filling – affair, head here on a Saturday afternoon to tuck into a beautifully satisfying traditional roast.

Map 3 B3 **Metro** Dubai Marina

Nobu
Atlantis The Palm, Palm Jumeirah

Japanese
04 426 2626

Nobuyuki Matsuhisa has upped the ante for sushi in the city. Japanese food aficionados will love the exceptional quality, attention to detail and huge menu of sushi, sashimi and tempura. It's recommended to book ahead.

Map 1 C1 **Metro** Nakheel

The Observatory
Dubai Marriott Harbour Hotel & Suites,
 Dubai Marina

International

04 319 4795

It's all about the view at this atmospheric 52nd floor gastro-lounge. Spectacular 360° vistas over the Marina and The Palm accompany the concise (but tasty) menu, while the cocktails are excellent. Arrive before sunset then stay for the evening to enjoy the panorama in full.

Map 3 B1 **Metro** Dubai Marina

Okku
The Monarch Dubai, Trade Centre 1

Japanese
04 501 8777

There's more than enough to make you go 'mmm!' at Okku: the trendy decor, so very low lighting, great food and even greater, cocktail-fuelled party nights out. If prices are ever a sign of substance, then it definitely drives the point home, but its menu of sushi, sashimi and tempura is so fancifully executed that you may have to agree. Take the luxury up a notch and book one of the chic tatami rooms for private dining. Alternatively, just turn up at the weekend to sip cocktails in the bar. **Map** 2 E1 **Metro** World Trade Centre

Okku

Ossiano

Seafood

Atlantis The Palm, Palm Jumeirah   04 426 2626

Three Michelin star chef Santi Santamaria serves up Catalan-inspired simple, delicate seafood dishes at this impeccable eatery. Glistening chandeliers and floor-to-ceiling views of the enormous Ambassador Lagoon provides a formal, but romantic, setting to enjoy the seafood creations.

Map 1 C1 **Metro** Nakheel

Pachanga

Latin American

Hilton Dubai Jumeirah Resort, Dubai Marina   04 318 2530

Choose from the Havana-style bar, Brazilian barbecue, Mexican lounge or Argentinean terrace that surround the dancefloor at this hotspot. Start with fresh guacamole prepared at your table, then move onto the wide selection of mains: the seafood is delicious but the real winners are meat-eaters. Wednesday is tango night.

Map 3 A1 **Metro** Jumeirah Lakes Towers

Pai Thai

Thai

Al Qasr, Al Sufouh 1   04 366 6730

You'll have a night to remember at Pai Thai, from the abra ride to the restaurant to the novel Thai cuisine. If you are lucky, at some point in the evening you will be entertained by a traditionally dressed Thai dancer whose precise movements are as impressive as the food on your beautifully set table. The outdoor seating area is delightful and the menu provides the odd twist on familiar favourites.

Map 3 E1 **Metro** Mall Of The Emirates

Peppercrab

Pars Iranian Kitchen

Persian

Nr Chelsea Plaza Hotel, Al Jafiliya   04 398 4000

Pars offers a traditional laid-back atmosphere a million miles from the modernity suggested by its neon sign. The menu includes a selection of grilled meats, kebabs and Iranian stews. Its delightful front garden, enclosed by a fairy light-entwined hedgerow, is home to low tables and soft, majlis bench seats; perfect for enjoying a leisurely shisha.

Map 1 H2 **Metro** Al Jafiliya

Peppercrab

Singaporean

Grand Hyatt Dubai, Umm Hurair 2   04 317 2222

One of Dubai's many Asian restaurants, Peppercrab stands out thanks to its Singaporean theme. The noodles and chilli

crab are authentic enough to make you feel like you're sitting in the middle of Clark's Quay in the Lion City. Also loyal to the fabulously tasty Singaporean cooking traditions, the menu's many Malay notes add welcome variety on your plate.

Map 4 B6 **Metro** Healthcare City

Pierchic
Seafood

Al Qasr, Al Sufouh 1
04 366 6730

Pierchic has the best location of any Dubai restaurant. Perched at the end of a long wooden pier that juts into the Arabian Gulf, it affords front-row seats of an unobstructed Burj Al Arab, as well as Dubai Marina and Palm Jumeirah in the distance. The delicately presented seafood and famed wine list come at a price but what you're really paying for is the view, especially if you request a table on the terrace. A good spot for romantic occasions.

Map 3 E1 **Metro** Mall Of The Emirates

Ravi's
Pakistani

Nr Satwa R/A, Al Satwa Rd, Al Satwa
04 331 5353

This much-loved diner offers a range of Pakistani curry favourites, rice dishes and freshly baked naan bread, alongside more adventurous fare such as fried brains. The setting is basic, but that hasn't stopped Ravi's from gaining cult status among local expats. Most people opt to sit outside with all of Satwa life on show, but dining is also available in the main restaurant or in the quieter family section. Either way, it's the food that really excels: you can eat like a king for under Dhs.30. **Map** 1 H2 **Metro** Al Jafiliya

Reem Al Bawadi

Arabic/Lebanese

Nr HSBC, Jumeira Rd, Jumeira 3   04 394 7444

Semi-isolated booths with thick Arabic cushions line the walls, while tables lined with armchairs fill the dark, bustling dining area. Reem Al Bawadi's mostly-Arab clientele is a good sign that the grills and mezze coming out of its kitchen are authentic. The Dubai Marina branch (04 452 2525) is a good choice for a similar experience in that end of town.

Map 1 G2 **Metro** Burj Khalifa/Dubai Mall

Rhodes Mezzanine

British

Grosvenor House, Dubai Marina   04 399 8888

The sleek, airy setting of this upscale eatery lets the food take centre stage and the creations by Gary Rhodes are easily up to the task: exquisite British cooking with a French twist is what's on offer, and the standard of cooking is such that even a mac n' cheese gets transformed into a Michelin-worthy dish.

Map 3 B1 **Metro** Dubai Marina

Rococo

Italian

Sofitel Dubai Jumeirah Beach, Dubai Marina   04 448 4848

Rococo's interior could be described as fusion – the chandeliers resemble upside down cocktail glasses, the floors are black marble, the ceiling is a white swirling design, the side walls are deep purple, and there's a sea-view from the large windows. The menu leans towards a more classic, Italian palate, with a sprinkling of interesting twists by the Umbrian chef. Tucked away in the Sofitel hotel, this is one of the gems in JBR. **Map** 3 A1 **Metro** Jumeirah Lakes Towers

Restaurants & Cafes

Ronda Locatelli

Italian

Atlantis The Palm, Palm Jumeirah   04 426 2626

An off-shoot of London's famed Locanda Locatelli, this restaurant features tables surrounding the centrepiece of the room: a huge stone-built wood-fired pizza oven. The casual menu offers a large selection of starters, pasta and mains, as well as a range of small dishes for sharing. Prices are quite reasonable for such a connected restaurant.

Map 1 C1 **Metro** Nakheel

Rostang

French

Atlantis The Palm, Palm Jumeirah   04 426 2626

Rostang's wood trim, leather bench seating and dim lighting perfectly mimic the decor of a French bistro from the 1930s. The food is just as reminiscent. Two-star Michelin chef Michel Rostang's seafood-heavy menu is hardly simple, but full of comforting dishes that shy away from experimentation and concentrate on preparation and presentation.

Map 1 C1 **Metro** Nakheel

Ruth's Chris Steak House

Steakhouse

The H Hotel, Trade Centre 1   04 501 8666

Ruth's Chris is an international institution among carnivores with a flair for fine fare, and the Dubai branch delivers on the high expectations. White leather sofas, red and dark panelling and slick service are topped off with superior steaks, served with a superb selection of accompaniments. A second branch is located at the Address hotel in Dubai Marina (04 454 9538).

Map 2 E1 **Metro** World Trade Centre

Ronda Locatelli

Sahn Eddar

Burj Al Arab, Umm Suqeim 3

Afternoon Tea
04 301 7600

Those with normal-sized pockets won't get a better opportunity to inspect the Burj Al Arab. This is where you can slurp tea and nibble expensive scones at the base of the world's tallest atrium. There's an endless feast of delicious sandwiches, scones, cakes, sweets and a pot of your choice of the finest teas. After, consider a drink at the Skyview Bar for the stunning vistas 200m above the sea.

Map 3 E1 **Metro** Mall Of The Emirates

Salmontini Le Resto

Mall Of The Emirates, Al Barsha 1

Seafood
04 341 0222

Salmontini's chic interior is fashioned around large windows overlooking the mall's indoor ski slope. Choose from a selection of Scottish salmon, worked in every possible way (from smoked and grilled to cured and poached). All-inclusive deals offered during the week make a night here more cost-effective.

Map 3 E2 **Metro** Mall Of The Emirates

Saravana Bhavan

Nr Karama Park Square, Al Karama

Indian
04 334 5252

Taking its name from a much-loved hotel in Chennai, this unassuming joint is arguably the best of the area's south Indian restaurants. The menu is long enough to keep Indian expats interested but it's the thalis that draw crowds. For around Dhs.10 you can get a plate packed with colour and flavours, dal and chapatti. Fine Indian food doesn't come much cheaper. **Map** 4 B3 **Metro** Al Karama

Seafire Steakhouse & Bar

Steakhouse
04 426 2626

Atlantis The Palm, Palm Jumeirah

The warm colours at Seafire contrast nicely with the rest of
Atlantis, while the smell of leather and cosy alcoves conspire
to create the vibe of something well-established. Seafood
and steak dominate the menu, all of it expertly prepared,
and the signature dessert, a trio of chocolate treats, is worth
waiting for.

Map 1 C1 **Metro** Nakheel

Segreto

Italian
04 366 6730

Dar Al Masyaf, Al Sufouh 1

Segreto is tucked away from the more bustling parts of Souk
Madinat Jumeirah, and once inside, its smooth lines, pristine
presentation and warm sandy tones give the experience a
soothing start. Your dining journey can begin with sweet
champagne cocktails and delicious breads. The food is
aesthetically appealing, but the portions are more suited to a
catwalk model than a prop forward.

Map 3 E1 **Metro** Mall Of The Emirates

Shabestan

Persian

Radisson Blu Hotel, Dubai Deira Creek, Al Rigga   04 222 7171

This restaurant is as much about the decor as it is about
the food. Ornate tables and chairs, decorative trinkets
and traditional cooking stations combine to give a regal
experience. The freshly baked breads epitomise the quality of
food and the dishes are plentiful.

Map 4 D2 **Metro** Union

Shang Palace

Chinese

Shangri-La Hotel, Trade Centre 1 — 04 405 2703

Shang Palace's food is delicious and the attentive staff are available to guide newcomers through the numerous options. Familiar dishes are well prepared, and set menus are available. With shark fin soup, live seafood and dim sum, this is certainly a place for something different. A well-stocked bar makes this a suitable venue to start an evening.

Map 2 C1 **Metro** Financial Centre

Spectrum On One

International

Fairmont Dubai, Trade Centre 1 — 04 311 8316

With probably the most diverse menu in Dubai, Spectrum On One caters for a variety of tastes throughout each course.

The menu takes at least a half hour to read and features both adventurous and familiar dishes from southern Asia, coastal Thailand, Japan, India and Europe. For an excellent-value option, you can taste them all in a few hours at the fabulous champagne brunch on Fridays.

Map 2 E1 **Metro** World Trade Centre

Going Out

Splendido Restaurant
Italian

The Ritz-Carlton Dubai, Dubai Marina   04 399 4000

Head to Splendido for an extensive menu featuring excellent, classic Italian fare. Tasty mains and delicious desserts are all generously portioned, while the overall tone is quietly classy and pleasantly pleasing. There's also a good wine list with plenty of all-Italian favourites to delight discerning diners. To top it up, the hotel's enviable location on the JBR beach provides a great opportunity to take a casual stroll along the beach after your meal.

Map 3 A1 **Metro** Dubai Marina

Sultan's Lounge
Cafe

Jumeirah Zabeel Saray, Palm Jumeirah   04 453 0444

The interior section of Sultan's Lounge is finely appointed for a Turkish-themed hangout, but really the outlet is made by the large, relaxed terrace that is perfect for chilling out under the stars during the cooler months. Sandwiches and light bites dominate the menu, with the real immensity of variety reserved for the teas, coffees and other drinks. The lovely English or Ottoman afternoon teas are a must here.

Map 1 C2 **Metro** Nakheel

Spectrum on One

Restaurants & Cafes

Sumibiya
Korean

Radisson Blu Hotel, Dubai Deira Creek, Al Rigga   04 222 7171

Eating is a social affair at this yakiniku (Korean grilled meat) eatery, where diners entertain themselves using the gas grill in the middle of every table to sear, grill and charcoal bite-size morsels. It's informal, fun and tasty; if your food is overdone, you only have yourself to blame.

Map 4 D2 **Metro** Union

Table 9
International

Hilton Dubai Creek, Al Rigga   04 212 7551

Located in the space that once held Gordon Ramsay's Verre restaurant, Table 9 is a new British serving of fine dining. The menu offers a mix of traditional favourites such as venison and lobster, with a few less conventional dishes such as rabbit and pork knuckle to liven up the range. The portion sizes are perfect for sharing so you'll have the option to sample a wide variety of dishes. **Map** 4 D3 **Metro** Al Rigga

Tagine
Moroccan

The Palace At One&Only Royal Mirage,
  Al Sufouh 1   04 399 9999

Beneath ground level, through an enormous wooden door, past a majlis area draped in rich embroidery and perfumed with incense, you'll find the authentic Tagine. The low seating, arched alleys and courtyard setting, as well as the traditionally dressed waiters, create a traditional vibe as you sample the aromatic tagines and couscous creations.

Map 3 B1 **Metro** Nakheel

Teatro
International
Towers Rotana, Trade Centre 1 — 04 312 2202

For awesome views of Sheikh Zayed Road served up with fantastic food, head to Teatro. The creative menus will please most diners, with standard Japanese fare alongside palate pleasers such as fresh pasta with lobster. Trendy design features and an impressive wine cellar complete the picture.

Map 2 C1 **Metro** Financial Centre

The Thai Kitchen
Thai
Park Hyatt Dubai, Port Saeed — 04 317 2222

Intertwined around four live-cooking areas where all the ingredients are displayed and prepared, Thai Kitchen is a slick, contemporary dining space. Thai food doesn't come fresher or more authentic on this side of Bangkok. With small, tapas-style portions at reasonable prices, your best bet is to order two or three per person and share. Finish it off by sipping a drink on the terrace which grants soothing views of the creek; or pop over to The Terrace (p.317) lounge next door.

Map 4 C5 **Metro** GGICO

Thiptara
Thai
The Palace – The Old Town, Downtown Dubai — 04 888 3444

Expect fresh and spicy seafood at this quality Thai restaurant overlooking the Burj Khalifa and lake. There's a lively lobster tank from which to take your pick, while the wine list is extensive. This is a hard location to beat for impressing visitors and business associates.

Map 2 B3 **Metro** Burj Khalifa/Dubai Mall

Tokyo@thetowers

Japanese

Boulevard At Jumeirah Emirates Towers,
  Trade Centre 2

04 319 8088

With elegantly partitioned tatami rooms, lively teppanyaki
tables and an eclectic menu, tokyo@thetowers offers diners
enough options to keep things interesting time after time.
The private rooms all have traditional floor cushions, or you
can choose to dine by the windows overlooking the mall.
Map 2 D2 **Metro** Emirates Towers

Toro Toro

Latin American

Grosvenor House, Dubai Marina

04 399 8888

Entering the pan-Latin eatery is like stepping into a dramatic
amphitheatre – giant bull sculptures flank the entrance and
a two-storey fireplace lights the foyer. The menu is divided
into three sections; from the sea, from the land and from the
garden. Dishes are served tapas-style and each delicately
prepared entree is served lovingly with influences from as far
as Brazil to Peru. **Map** 3 B1 **Metro** Dubai Marina

Trader Vic's

Polynesian

Souk Madinat Jumeirah, Al Sufouh 1

04 366 5646

Until you've experienced Trader Vic's, you can't consider
yourself a seasoned night-lifer. Delicious Asian-inspired dishes
and moreish snacks are available or you can jump straight
to the famously exotic cocktails, served in ceramic skulls and
seashells. Head to the Crowne Plaza branch (04 305 6399) for
live Cuban music every night.
Map 3 E1 **Metro** Mall Of The Emirates

Toro Toro

Traiteur

International

Park Hyatt Dubai, Port Saeed

04 317 2222

Having descended from an intimate bar via a dramatic
staircase, you'll be struck by the restaurant's soaring ceilings.
Traiteur's beautiful open kitchen then provides a great focal
point for the French and modern European cuisine.
Map 4 C5 **Metro** GGICO

Troyka

Russian

Ascot Hotel, Al Raffa

04 352 0900

Troyka's Russian-themed old world charm creates an
intimate mood to enjoy the hearty, tasty cuisines on offer.
The excellent-value Tuesday night buffet is all-inclusive
and comprises time-honoured delicacies from the Russian
kitchen. But food is not the only attraction here: if all you
need is a dose of bizarre entertainment, a band plays every
night from 22:30 and Vegas-style cabaret begins soon after.
Map 4 B2 **Metro** Al Fahidi

Villa Beach

International

Jumeirah Beach Hotel, Umm Suqeim 3

04 406 8999

The buggy ride to the restaurant's door reveals the killer
attraction: you're a bun's throw from the ocean and the Burj
Al Arab. The beach-hut aesthetic has a Polynesian vibe but
the food is mostly modern Mediterranean. The service is
excellent, and although the scenery doesn't come cheap, the
food is beautifully prepared and the wine list has been put
together with care. **Map** 3 E1 **Metro** Mall Of The Emirates

GOVERNMENT OF DUBAI

DUBAI DOLPHINARIUM

DUBAI MUNICIPALITY

Live Dolphin & Seal Show Timings
Mon to Thu - 11am & 6pm ; Fri & Sat - 11am, 3pm & 6pm
Swim sessions with Dolphins: Mon to Thu - 1pm to 4pm
Celebrate your Birthday at Dubai Dolphinarium

Location: Creek Park, Gate 1, Dubai, Call: +971 4 336 9773
Toll Free: 800-DOLPHIN (800-3657446)
Book your tickets online at www.dubaidolphinarium.ae

Our Vision: To Create an excellent city that provides the essence of success and comfort of living.

Vivaldi
Italian

Sheraton Dubai Creek Hotel & Towers, Al Rigga   04 207 1750

Located on the sparkling Deira Creek in the heart of old Dubai, Vivaldi's setting makes this Italian eatery a contender for one of the most romantic restaurants in town. Spectacular creekside views from both inside and out on the two lovely terraces set the scene, and an novel Italian menu – as well as a comprehensive wine list – complete the picture.

Map 4 D3 **Metro** Union

Vu's
Mediterranean

Jumeirah Emirates Towers, Trade Centre 2   04 319 8088

A stylish and elegant eatery, this is fine dining at its best and with one of the most sensational views in town. The menu is finely compiled with dishes certain to impress: you can start with caviar linguine and move on to the signature dishes of lobster or roast pigeon. Each plate is exquisitely presented and it's often worth a trip for the cocktails alone.

Map 2 D2 **Metro** Emirates Towers

Wagamama
Japanese

Al Fattan Towers, JBR, Dubai Marina   04 399 5900

Perched above The Walk and modelled on a traditional Japanese ramen bar, with communal tables, Wagamama is a good option for a quick bite in JBR. Orders are immediately and freshly prepared; if you want to linger over your meal, it's wise to order a course at a time. Other branches are located in Crowne Plaza (04 305 6060) and The Greens (04 361 5757).

Map 3 A1 **Metro** Jumeirah Lakes Towers

West 14th New York Grill & Bar
Steakhouse
Oceana Beach Club, Palm Jumeirah · 04 447 7601

It may be at the Oceana Beach Club but, make no mistake, West 14th is not the kind of place you turn up to in shorts and flip-flops. This Brooklyn-inspired, warehouse-style steakhouse is all about indulgence, from the comfy red leather armchairs to the oversized meat portions and the 12+ signature caipirinhas.

Map 1 C1 **Metro** Nakheel

Yalumba
International
Le Meridien Dubai, Al Garhoud · 04 702 2328

Famous for its raucous Friday bubbly buffets, this Australian restaurant doesn't limit itself to steak. Head there for the Thursday night buffet with unlimited champagne, sushi, stir-fry, seafood, steak and more desserts than you can possibly manage. Wednesdays feature an Aussie barbecue where you can even throw your own shrimps on. Just leave your board shorts at home.

Map 4 E6 **Metro** GGICO

Yo! Sushi
Japanese
Dubai Marina Mall, Dubai Marina · 04 399 7708

This cheerful chain specialises in serving up sushi and other unashamedly stereotypical Japanese bites in a fun setting. The Marina branch is no exception; grab a table at the bar to sample the small portions transported around on a conveyor belt. Other branches include DIFC (04 363 7404) and Mirdif (04 284 3995). **Map** 3 A1 **Metro** Jumeirah Lakes Towers

Zafran
Indian

Dubai Marina Mall, Dubai Marina   04 399 7357

As far as mall-eats go, Zafran stands apart – Michelin-starred chef Atul Kochars is behind the venture and you can look forward to some superbly tasty Indian creations. There's another branch in Mirdif City Centre (04 284 0987).

Map 3 A1 **Metro** Jumeirah Lakes Towers

Zheng He's
Chinese

Mina A'Salam, Al Sufouh 1   04 366 6730

Zheng He's superb take on Chinese delicacies, together with the restaurant's exquisite waterside spot in Souk Madinat Jumeirah, ensure a constant stream of patrons. The dim sum and mini-roll starters are divine, while the marinated fish, stir-fried style meat and duck are all worth discovering as well. The wine list is as thick as it is pricey, but in terms of culinary experience you certainly get what you pay for.

Map 3 E2 **Metro** Mall Of The Emirates

Zuma
Japanese

Dubai International Financial Centre (DIFC), Trade Centre 2   04 425 5660

Since its opening, Zuma has gained a firm following as one of Dubai's best restaurants. The stunning space is elegantly lit, with clean lines of wood and glass to set the scene. The food that arrives from the open kitchen and sushi bar is presented in classic Japanese style – it is all about simplicity and flair here, with prices to match. If dinner is beyond your budget, opt for a drink at the bar. **Map** 2 C2 **Metro** Emirates Towers

Zheng He's

Bars, Pubs & Clubs

Sky-high cocktail lounges, beachside bars and enough clubs to keep you dancing for a year all jostle for your evening attention.

360°
Bar

Jumeirah Beach Hotel, Umm Suqeim 3   04 406 8999

One visit to this Umm Suqeim hottie is enough to convince you that this is what holidays were made for: like a static carousel for grown-ups, 360° is a circular rooftop with a bar at its heart. The place boasts stunning panoramic views of the Arabian Gulf. Early arrivals (it opens at 17:00 and 16:00 on Friday) can take their pick of low white couches and suck whichever colourful shisha they fancy. Sunset signals cocktails, beats and one of the city's best alfresco nights.
Map 3 E1 **Metro** Mall Of The Emirates

The Agency
Bar

Souk Madinat Jumeirah, Al Sufouh 1   04 366 6320

With a veritable vineyard of the squashed grape on offer, even wine connoisseurs won't fail to find something quaffable on the 30 page wine menu. Dark wood, exposed brickwork and perch-friendly seating complete the chic setting. Tasty tapas-style bites include spring rolls, spicy prawns and delicious olives. There's another branch in Emirates Towers which has a more extensive food menu.
Map 3 E1 **Metro** Mall Of The Emirates

360°

Bahri Bar

Bar

Mina A'Salam, Al Sufouh 1   04 366 6730

Imagine you had the chance to design the perfect bar. For starters you'd include a stunning view, with windtower rooftops, rustling palm trees, meandering canals, the towering Burj Al Arab and sparkling ocean beyond. The bar could have rich furnishings, comfortable seating and ornately engraved lanterns. On the menu you'd make sure a comprehensive cocktail selection was accompanied by wines, beers, and delicious nibbles. Welcome to Bahri Bar.

Map 3 E1 **Metro** Mall Of The Emirates

Bar 44
Bar

Grosvenor House, Dubai Marina 04 399 8888

At Bar 44 waiters with waistcoats that match the bar's carpets whizz around with expensive bottles of champagne, a jazz singer swoons impressively at a grand piano, and plumes of (pricey) cigar smoke fill the air. The cocktails are equally regal and you get to enjoy it all to a backdrop of some great Marina views. **Map** 3 B1 **Metro** Dubai Marina

Barasti
Bar

Le Meridien Mina Seyahi Beach Resort &
  Marina, Al Sufouh 1 04 399 3333

Barasti is a Dubai nightlife institution. The sprawling beachside venue features inviting loungers and daybeds, a downstairs bar and big screens for the all-important events on the sporting scene, along with heaps of casual charm and plenty of revelling party-goers. This laid-back bar is a firm expat favourite, loved for its meaty menu, jugs of Pimms and panoramic vistas, not to mention the fact you can turn up in flip-flops or Friday finery depending on your mood.
Map 3 B1 **Metro** Dubai Marina

Barzar
Bar

Souk Madinat Jumeirah, Al Sufouh 1 04 366 6730

The upper level of this slick two-floor bar is open in the middle so you can peer over at the band and drinkers below. The overall vibe is relaxed and urban, complete with eclectic drinks such as beer cocktails (champagne with Guinness) and traditional long drinks. **Map** 3 E1 **Metro** Mall Of The Emirates

Belgian Beer Cafe
Pub

Crowne Plaza Dubai Festival City, Festival City   04 701 1127

Aside from the namesake beverage, the main draws are the moules frites; mussels served in your choice of sauce with crisp fries and lots of bread for mopping up the juices. Fittingly for a Belgian joint, the beer selection is top notch, if a tad on the expensive side. The traditional dining room fills up fast, as does the terrace, and the views are second to none.

Map 1 J4 **Metro** Emirates

BidiBondi
Bar

Clubhouse Al Manhal, Shoreline Apartments,
 Palm Jumeirah   04 427 0515

This laid-back offering on Palm Jumeirah offers indoor and alfresco space, with a beach diner and Aussie-style hangout lounge. There is a great range of mocktails, cocktails, beers and wines to choose from, and, should you get hungry, the food menu offers hefty burgers, sandwiches and salads plus bar snacks. Breakfast is also available for the morning after.

Map 3 C1 **Metro** Nakheel

Blends
Bar

The Address Dubai Marina, Dubai Marina   04 436 7777

Blends is a popular hangout among Dubai Marina locals looking for a night out on the town. Arrive early to secure one of the plush armchairs before revelling party-goers take over the small dance floor area. An extensive drinks list lubricates the atmosphere and there's a separate cigar lounge.

Map 3 A1 **Metro** Dubai Marina

Blue Bar

Bar

Novotel World Trade Centre Dubai, Trade Centre 2   04 332 0000

Jazz fans unite for some of the best live music in town. Hidden at the back of the Novotel, the Blue Bar has a relaxed, low-key vibe with enough 'it' factor to give it street cred but without any delusions of grandeur. You can opt to either pull up a stool at the large square bar, or get cosy on one of the leather sofas and armchairs.

Map 2 E2 **Metro** World Trade Centre

Boudoir

Nightclub

Dubai Marine Beach Resort & Spa, Jumeira 1   04 345 5995

This exclusive spot can be as difficult to get into as a lady's chamber but once you get past the doormen – as long as you are appropriately dressed – you will be treated to a Parisian-style club that's perfect for dangerous liaisons. The regular free drinks for ladies help pack the circular dance floor.

Map 1 H2 **Metro** Al Jafiliya

Buddha Bar

Bar

Grosvenor House, Dubai Marina   04 399 8888

Buddha Bar has the wow factor. From the entrance, a seductively lit corridor leads you past private lounges and tucked-away alcoves; all perfectly decadent places to dine, lounge, and socialise. With the Buddha Bar's famous mix of music, some of the best cocktails in town and a selection of tasty Asian treats, this Grosvenor House (p.70) haunt is a firm favourite among Dubai's army of socialites.

Map 3 B1 **Metro** Dubai Marina

Clockwise from top left: Double Decker, Barzar, Cavalli Club

Calabar
Bar

The Address Downtown Dubai, Downtown Dubai   04 436 8888

A large, sweeping bar serving cigars and all manner of drinks from international brews to Latin cocktails is the centrepiece of this chic lounge. There's also a decent selection of nibbles and the terrace offers spectacular views of the Burj Khalifa.

Map 2 B3 **Metro** Burj Khalifa/Dubai Mall

Caramel Restaurant & Lounge
Bar

Dubai International Financial Centre (DIFC),
Trade Centre 2   04 425 6677

This is a place where those who work hard come to play in a similar manner. Oozing urban cool, the stylish restaurant spills out from the bar through open walls on to the terrace, where cabanas set the mood for stylish lounging. In addition to an extensive selection of drinks, there's a menu of light bites and nibbles to keep hunger at bay. During the day, Caramel turns into one of the more stylish spots for lunch around DIFC.

Map 2 C2 **Metro** Financial Centre

Cavalli Club
Nightclub

Fairmont Dubai, Trade Centre 1   04 332 9260

Roberto Cavalli's leopard print and Swarovski encrusted nightspot is one of the city's places to be seen if you're part of the 'it' crowd. It's all suitably decadent and as unashamedly over the top as can be expected from the Italian designer. There's also a cocktail and cigar lounge, wine bar and even a boutique shop to enjoy – if you can get through the door.

Map 2 E1 **Metro** World Trade Centre

Chi@The Lodge
Nightclub

Al Nasr Leisureland, Oud Metha   04 337 9470

The Lodge is always busy with its indoor and outdoor dancefloors, lots of seating and large screens and VIP cabanas. The regular theme nights with fancy dress are popular, especially the legendary 'cheese'. On top of all that, it's easy to get taxis outside, there's often a shawarma stand in the carpark and entrance is free before 22:00 on most nights.

Map 4 B4 **Metro** Oud Metha

Dhow & Anchor
Pub

Jumeirah Beach Hotel, Umm Suqeim 3   04 406 8999

Dhow & Anchor's bar is a popular spot, particularly during happy hour and sporting events – try the outdoor terrace if you are dining and enjoy glimpses of the Burj Al Arab. The menu includes the usual range of drinks and terrific curries, roast dinners, pies, and fish and chips.

Map 3 E1 **Metro** Mall Of The Emirates

Double Decker
Pub

Al Murooj Rotana, Trade Centre 2   04 321 1111

On a Friday afternoon this could be your average pub in just any town around the world. With big screen sports, dangerously long happy hours and karaoke, many appreciate the relative charms this pub provides. Fridays are the most crowded thanks to the inexpensive boozy brunch. Somewhat refreshingly, there is little need to worry about dress code; trainers, flip-flops and shorts are all fine.

Map 2 C2 **Metro** Financial Centre

Eclipse Bar
Bar

InterContinental Dubai Festival City, Festival City   04 701 1111

On the 26th floor, Eclipse is all about glamour, with red leather padded walls, marble tables and a huge bar serving hundreds of different cocktails. It's also a great vantage point for cityscape views of Sheikh Zayed Road's high-rises.

Map 1 J4 **Metro** Emirates

Embassy Dubai
Nightclub

Grosvenor House, Dubai Marina   04 399 8888

In addition to a club and restaurant, this Grosvenor House venue boasts a vodka and champagne bar. The decor is opulent: intricately tiled walls, baroque lamps, candlelit tables and floor-to-ceiling windows overlooking the Dubai Marina skyline all add to the luxurious feel to make a decadent night out. **Map** 3 B1 **Metro** Dubai Marina

Healey's Bar & Terrace
Bar

Bonnington Jumeirah Lakes Towers,
Jumeirah Lakes Towers   04 356 0600

Wednesday night is the night at Healey's, which has a live DJ and three free drinks for women from 20:00 to 23:00. The stylish bar, with an ultra-chic glass bar, is perfect for glam patrons looking for a place to start the evening. Prop up at the bar and you can almost believe you are sipping cocktails in a Manhattan bar, and not in the middle of Jumeirah Lakes Towers. To top off the drama, head to the terrace, where you can sip cocktails outside surrounded by marina vistas.

Map 3 A2 **Metro** Jumeirah Lakes Towers

Top: The Irish Village, Bottom: Healey's Bar & Terrace

The Hub
Bar

Sofitel Dubai Jumeirah Beach, Dubai Marina   04 448 4848

A cut above your average sports bar, The Hub, located in the Sofitel hotel (04 448 4848), is a welcome addition to the JBR Walk. Ascend above the crowds and get ready to sample a decent selection of bottled and draught beers. Flat screen TVs show an array of sports and the buzzing atmosphere makes it a popular hangout. **Map** 3 A1 **Metro** Jumeirah Lakes Towers

The Irish Village
Pub

Nr Dubai Tennis Stadium, Al Garhoud   04 282 4750

The Irish Village is the nearest thing Dubai has to a beer garden, and the best place to go for fish and chips (complete with Guinness batter) and a pint of the dark stuff. Despite being one of the largest pubs in the city, this award-winning haunt is almost always packed with people looking to let their hair down while enjoying a bit of home nostalgia. Expect hearty pub food, twinkling lights in the trees and a live musician or two. **Map** 4 D6 **Metro** GGICO

Jambase
Bar

Souk Madinat Jumeirah, Al Sufouh 1   04 366 6730

Jambase's tempting selection of cocktails is enough to kick off a good night. There is an authentic 50s style jazz bar atmosphere created by the dark wooden interior and a live band kicking out the jams. The vaguely art deco stylings play host to completely contrasting evenings. Despite serving delicious food, it's best to arrive after 23:00 when the dancefloor fills up. **Map** 3 E1 **Metro** Mall Of The Emirates

Jetty Lounge

Bar

One&Only Royal Mirage, Al Sufouh 1   04 399 9999

This beachside bar manages to strike a great balance
between stylish and relaxed. Located in the exclusive
One&Only Royal Mirage (p.71), just steps from the hotel's
private beach, the loungy setting is perfect for sundowners:
park yourself on the comfy seats, kick back and get ready to
indulge in a few tasty snacks as you while away the evening
hours. You can also take a ferry to the hotel's sister property,
One&Only The Palm (p.76). **Map** 3 B1 **Metro** Nakheel

N'Dulge Nightclub

Nightclub

Atlantis The Palm, Palm Jumeirah   04 426 2626

Expect something special from Atlantis, like a suspended
catwalk in a nightclub – because that's what you get at
N'Dulge, along with lashings of cool. This space is modern,
glam and packed with hotel guests and dedicated clubbers
looking to let their hair down in style.
Map 1 C1 **Metro** Nakheel

Neos

Bar

The Address Downtown Dubai,
  Downtown Dubai   04 436 8888

Dubai is not short of bars with the wow-factor and Neos
definitely falls into this lofty bracket: take the lift to the 63rd
floor and get ready to be wowed by the views. With huge
wall-to-wall windows, Neos' staggering height makes it
hard to play it cool as you stare out at Burj Khalifa and the
city beyond. **Map** 2 B3 **Metro** Burj Khalifa/Dubai Mall

Nezesaussi Grill
Bar

Al Manzil Hotel, Downtown Dubai   04 428 5888

This upmarket sports bar, home to the best ribs in town, has enough glam to keep women happy while the match is on. Tastefully decked out in memorabilia, Nezesaussi might be a tongue-twister but once you've been there, the name is hard to forget. Although it boasts South African sausages, lamb from New Zealand and Australian steaks, it's not all beer and beef.

Map 2 B3 **Metro** Burj Khalifa/Dubai Mall

Oeno Wine Bar
Bar

The Westin Dubai Mina Seyahi Beach Resort &
  Marina, Al Sufouh 1   04 399 4141

Oeno's decor is modern and stylish, and the wine wall, complete with a librarian-style bookshelf ladder, adds a sense of decadence. There's a temperature-controlled cheese room with over 50 types of cheese, as well as a menu full of antipasti options. For an unbeatable date, book a table on the terrace.

Map 3 B1 **Metro** Nakheel

The Roof Top & Sports Lounge
Bar

One&Only Royal Mirage, Al Sufouh 1   04 399 9999

Clever design and lighting combine with a subtle DJ to make this one of Dubai's finest bars. Rooftop has a superb view of Palm Jumeirah, Moroccan decor with comfy majlis-style seating, intimate booths with huge cushions and a good menu of cocktails and bottled beers. If you're looking to kick back and relax under the stars there's no better place.

Map 3 B1 **Metro** Nakheel

Sanctuary Pool Lounge

Bar

Pullman Dubai Mall Of The Emirates, Al Barsha 1   04 377 2000

A chameleon of a location, head to Sanctuary's lofty poolside during the day to enjoy relaxed light bites and cocktails with a storming view of Dubai Marina, The Palm and Jumeira as a fitting backdrop while you soak up some rays. By night, Sanctuary has more of a chilled lounge ambience, serving up simple cuisine and cracking cocktails. Great for a quiet night with friends, or the first stop on a night out.

Map 3 E2 **Metro** Mall Of The Emirates

Shades

Bar

The Address Dubai Marina, Dubai Marina   04 436 7777

Located on the fourth floor of The Address Dubai Marina, Shades features white comfy sofas, making the pristine lounge a perfect hangout for pre-dinner drinks or shisha, although you can also tuck into BBQ fare here.

Map 3 A1 **Metro** Dubai Marina

Siddharta Lounge By Buddha Bar

Bar

Grosvenor House, Dubai Marina   04 399 8888

Ample lashings of plush white seating, gold accents and glam marble finishing set the scene at Siddharta. You'll be spoiled for choice with a posh snack menu that features a mouth-watering selection of Asian-Mediterranean specialities, including Wagyu beef mini burgers with orange soy and crispy prawn spring rolls with tamarind dipping sauce. Drinks aren't cheap, but this is a place to be seen.

Map 3 B1 **Metro** Dubai Marina

Sho Cho
Bar

Dubai Marine Beach Resort & Spa, Jumeira 1   04 346 1111

Sho Cho is a perfectly fine Japanese restaurant but that's not the real reason the beautiful set flock to its shoreline location. The sizeable bar, flanked by two alfresco eating areas and guarded by sharp-eyed waiters, is the real attraction. The tiny dancefloor is a poser's paradise; there's barely room to swing a man in tight jeans.

Map 1 H2 **Metro** World Trade Centre

Skyview Bar
Bar

Burj Al Arab, Umm Suqeim 3   04 301 7600

Come here in the evening for high-class cocktails and stunning views. Alternately, come for the afternoon tea and sit back, savouring the view while a waiter piles vast quantities of finger sandwiches, mini buns, cakes and biscuits on to your table, accompanied by a pot of tea and a glass of champagne. Book well in advance.

Map 3 E1 **Metro** Mall Of The Emirates

Trader Vic's Mai-Tai Lounge
Bar

Al Fattan Marine Tower II, JBR, Dubai Marina   04 399 8993

Perched above JBR Walk in Dubai Marina, this large bar is faithful to the iconic Trader Vic's style: decked out in Polynesian fixtures and fittings, Mai-Tai serves tropical cocktails, accompanied by tasty, if expensive, bar snacks. The spacious dancefloor provides a clubby feel should the cocktails put you in the mood to take a spin.

Map 3 A1 **Metro** Jumeirah Lakes Towers

Uptown Bar

The Terrace

Bar

Park Hyatt Dubai, Port Saeed

04 317 2222

Sweep through the Park Hyatt's atmospheric grounds and greenery, and you'll reach The Terrace: a haven of unhurried vibes and chillout tunes by the creek. Awash with contemporary white, chrome and wood, the interior extends out through shiny conservatory doors to an awning-adorned terrace. Scattered with couches and wooden tables, it's a gorgeous alfresco spot by the water. As far as chilled out terraces go, this is easily one of the most exclusive venues for sundowners in town. **Map** 4 C5 **Metro** GGICO

The Underground Pub

Pub

Habtoor Grand Beach Resort & Spa,
 Dubai Marina   04 399 5000

Themed on the London Tube, this popular sports pub in
Dubai Marina (p.104) is small and the compact space quickly
fills up during popular sporting events, when the pub's many
screens showing live sports pull in the crowds. There's also a
menu offering light bites and burgers, as well as a dartboard
and pool tables. **Map** 3 B1 **Metro** Dubai Marina

Uptown Bar

Bar

Jumeirah Beach Hotel, Umm Suqeim 3   04 406 8999

Take the lift to the 24th floor to find this small but perfectly
formed bar. The cool interior is classy enough, but Uptown's
selling point is the outdoor terrace: it's a perfect spot for
'sunset behind the Burj' photo ops. Get there at 18:00 to
take advantage of the half-price happy hour and cute little
canapes. **Map** 3 E1 **Metro** Mall Of The Emirates

Voda Bar

Bar

Jumeirah Zabeel Saray, Palm Jumeirah   04 453 0444

It's a bit of a trek to the outer fringes of The Palm, but if
Japanese nibbles and exotic cocktails tickle your fancy, a
cab ride to this sushi bar is well worth it. Located in the
extravagant Jumeirah Zabeel Saray hotel, Voda Bar has a
15-page list of Japanese-inspired cocktails – including the
refreshing Sake Highball – to sample over a platter of light
bites from the land of the rising sun.
Map 1 C2 **Metro** Nakheel

Warehouse

Bar

Le Meridien Dubai, Al Garhoud

04 702 2560

Warehouse's ground floor contains both an impressively stocked beer bar and well-rounded wine bar. Up the spiral staircase is a dual-personality restaurant – half fine dining and half sushi – where the food is elegantly displayed. As if that weren't enough, there's a vodka bar and a lounge club with an intimate dancefloor, DJ booth and just enough flash to warrant dressing up. **Map** 4 E6 **Metro** GGICO

Wavebreaker

Bar

Hilton Dubai Jumeirah Resort, Dubai Marina

04 399 1111

This popular beach bar at the Hilton Jumeirah (p.70) is the perfect place to spend a laidback afternoon by the sea; grab a drink and order a plate of nibbles to share while watching the sun go down. Later, the alfresco joint turns into an evening hangout with music, billiards and shisha.

Map 3 A1 **Metro** Jumeirah Lakes Tower

Zinc

Nightclub

Crowne Plaza Dubai, Trade Centre 1

04 331 1111

A slinky superclub experience awaits at Zinc: the soundtrack is modern R&B, house and hip-hop, with Housexy (Ministry of Sound) and Kinky Malinki ferrying over their rotas of UK DJs. Design-wise there are shiny flatscreens, lounge areas and glitzy mirrored walls, as well as a big dancefloor sectioned off by a mammoth bar. All combined, the elements mean that every night is a party night at this Crowne Plaza haunt.

Map 2 D1 **Metro** Emirates Towers

Index

Index

Explorer Products

Residents' Guides

Mini Visitors' Guides

Photography Books & Calendars

Maps

Adventure & Lifestyle Guides

Explorer Team

Check out askexplorer.com

Publishing
Founder & CEO Alistair MacKenzie
Associate Publisher Claire England

Editorial
Managing Editor – Consumer Carli Allan
Guides Editor Jo Iivonen
Managing Editor – Corporate
Charlie Scott
Deputy Corporate Editor Lily Lawes
Digital Projects Editor
Rachel McArthur
Web Editor Laura Coughlin
Production Manager Therese Theron
Production Assistant Vanessa Eguia
Editorial Assistant Amapola Castillo
Researchers Farida, Jagadeesh,
Shalu M Sukumar, Suchitra P

Design & Photography
Creative Director Pete Maloney
Art Director Ieyad Charaf
Contract Publishing Manager
Chris Goldstraw
Designer Michael Estrada
Junior Designers Didith Hapiz,
M. Shakkeer
Layout Manager Jayde Fernandes
Layout Designers Mansoor Ahmed,
Shawn Zuzarte
Cartography Manager
Zainudheen Madathil
Cartographer Noushad Madathil,
Jithesh Kalathingal, Hidayath Razi
GIS Analyst Rafi KM, Gayathri CM
Photography Manager Pamela Grist
Photographer Bart Wojcinski

Sales & Marketing
Group Media Sales Manager
Peter Saxby
Media Sales Area Managers
Adam Smith, Bryan Anes, Laura Zuffova,
Louise Burton, Matthew Whitbread,
Sabrina Ahmed
Media Sales Area Executive
Elliot Macnay
Digital Sales Area Manager
James Gaubert
Business Development Manager
Pouneh Hafizi
Corporate Solutions Account Manager
Vibeke Nurgberg
Group Marketing & PR Manager
Lindsay West
Senior Marketing Executive
Stuart L. Cunningham
Sales & Marketing Assistant
Shedan Ebona
Group Retail Sales Manager
Ivan Rodrigues
Retail Sales Coordinator
Michelle Mascarenhas
Retail Sales Area Supervisors
Ahmed Mainodin, Firos Khan
Retail Sales Merchandisers
Johny Mathew, Shan Kumar
Retail Sales Drivers Najumudeen K.I.,
Shabsir Madathil, Sujeer Khan
Warehouse Assistant Mohamed Haji

Finance, HR & Administration
Administration Manager
Fiona Hepher
Accountant Cherry Enriquez
Accounts Assistants Jeanette Carino
Enecillo, Joy Bermejo Belza, Sunil Suvarna
Admin Assistant & Reception
Joy H. San Buenaventura
Public Relations Officer Rafi Jamal
Office Assistant Shafeer Ahamed
Office Manager – India Jithesh Kalathingal

IT & Digital Solutions
Digital Solutions Manager
Derrick Pereira
IT Manager R. Ajay
Database Programmer Pradeep T.P.

Useful Numbers

Dubai Municipality	04 221 5555/800 900
Tourist Security Department	800 4438
Dubai Police (Emergency)	999
Fire Department	997
Ambulance	999
American Hospital	04 377 6644
Medcare Hospital	04 407 9111
Life Pharmacy (24 Hour)	04 344 1122
UAE Country Code	+971
Dubai Area Code	04
Directory Enquiries	181/199
International Operator Assistance	100
Weather Updates	04 216 2218

Airport Info

Emirates Airline	600 55 55 55
flydubai	231 1000
Dubai International Airport:	
Help Desk	04 224 5555
Flight Information	04 216 6666
Baggage Services	04 224 5383

Taxi Companies

Arabia Taxis	04 285 5566
Dubai Taxi	04 208 0808
Cars Taxis	800 227 789
Metro Taxis	600 566 000
National Taxis	600 543 322

Contact Us

▶ Website
Check out our new website for event listings, competitions and information on your city, and other cities in the Middle East.
Log onto ask**explorer**.com

▶ Newsletter
Register online to receive Explorer's weekly newsletter and be first in line for our special offers and competitions.
Log onto ask**explorer**.com

▶ General Enquiries
We'd love to hear your thoughts and answer any questions you have about this book or any other Explorer product.
Contact us at info@ask**explorer**.com

▶ Careers
If you fancy yourself as an Explorer, send your CV (stating the position you're interested in) to jobs@ask**explorer**.com

▶ Contract Publishing
For enquiries about Explorer's Contract Publishing arm and design services contact contracts@ask**explorer**.com

▶ Maps
For cartography enquiries, including orders and comments, contact maps@ask**explorer**.com

▶ Advertising and Corporate Sales
For bulk sales and customisation options, for this book or any Explorer product, contact sales@ask**explorer**.com